FILMED IN
BROOKLYN

MARGO DONOHUE

THE
History
PRESS

Published by The History Press
Charleston, SC
www.historypress.com

Front cover, clockwise from top left: Coney Island summer boardwalk, 2021; Radha Blank, 2020. *Courtesy of Jeong Park/Netflix*; Scarlett Johansson, 2019. *Courtesy of Netflix*; André Holland and Rebecca Hall, 2021. *Courtesy of Emily V. Aragones/Netflix*; Al Pacino, Martin Scorsese and Rodrigo Prieto, 2019. *Courtesy of Niko Tavernise/Netflix*.
Back cover, top to bottom: *War of the Worlds* house, 2021; Spike Lee mural, 2021; Richard Schenkman and Adam Beckman, 1998. *Courtesy of Tom Legoff*; Joker Art on Smith Street, 2022.

All images are by the author unless otherwise noted.

First published 2022

Manufactured in the United States

ISBN 9781467146760

Library of Congress Control Number: 2022939473

Notice: The information in this book is true and complete to the best of our knowledge. It is offered without guarantee on the part of the author or The History Press. The author and The History Press disclaim all liability in connection with the use of this book.

CONTENTS

ACKNOWLEDGEMENTS

This book in your hands starts with my good friend Margo Porras, my cohost on the *Book Vs. Movie* podcast and the author of *Growing Up in La Colonia: Boomer Memories from Oxnard's Barrio*. Margo put me in touch with the editors at The History Press for my first idea, a book about the neighborhood of Park Slope (still one of my dream projects to cover!). There, my excellent editor Banks Smither guided me to the idea of uncovering the entire borough of Brooklyn and its relationship to the film world. (Thank you so much for your support and patience with this first-time author!)

Winding around the web, the Brooklyn Library archives, IMDb (totally worth the membership), newspapers.com, Facebook groups and the recollections of my friends, I have uncovered the beginning of movie studios on an acre of land in Midwood in 1897 and the varying neighborhoods throughout the borough that make up the pastiche of America from its inception to the present day. I strove for veracity on every page, and I did my best to ensure the featured locations were accurate.

For some, I was only able to determine the neighborhoods they used for filming. When I could pinpoint an exact address, I included it. If I missed any, please reach out to me via email at brooklynfitchick@gmail.com, on Twitter or Instagram @BrooklynFitChick and through my website (www. brooklynfitchick.com). You can find my TikTok videos at @margodonohue.

I want to give a shout-out to my fellow writers who were generous with their time telling me about their favorite films shot in Brooklyn: Margo Porras, Kevin Powell, Kristen Meinzer, Gene Seymour, Sonia Mansfield,

Patrick Bromley, Adam Riske, Alicia Mintz, Robyn Buckley and Robert DiCristino. Check out their podcasts: *Book Vs. Movie, Dorking Out, F This Movie!, Movie Therapy with Rafer & Kristen, NPR Pop Culture Happy Hour* and *Trashy Divorces*.

There is no way I could have put this book together without images. The following places, people and outlets were vital to my search: the amazing public relations department at Netflix, Wikimedia, Creative Common Attribution (CCA is a tremendous resource!), the Brooklyn Public Library, the Brooklyn Historical Society, Alamy and Nixon Thelusmond.

Thank you to Lee Grant, Paul Bernstein, Richard Schenkman and Mary Lukasiewicz for speaking with me about your expertise in filmmaking and shooting in Brooklyn.

Deep gratitude to the best writers' group imaginable: Becky Randel, Alisha Gaddis, Claire Chase, Angelica Florio, Katya Lidsky, Mary Lukasiewicz, Salma Khan and Laura Kindred (my fellow TSBs!). You are all gems.

I would not be here without the support of my family and friends, including Moksha and Patrick; Kim and David; Patty and Barry; Hyatt and Hart; Laura; Julietta and Nick; Deborah and Candy; Jenn and Kristen; Michelle and Deb; Trish; Cristina; Cher (RIP Mamacita!); Lisa Mack; Brandi (Tofutti!); Lisa and Mike; Jenny; Kate; and all of my friends/students from Body Elite and the YMCA at the Armory. It was a pleasure to create playlists for you. The wisest teachers learn from their students! (Miss you, Mom, Dad, John and Joe.)

Special thanks to all my listeners for the *Book Vs. Movie, Dorking Out, Not Fade Away* and *What a Creep* podcasts. You make all the work a pleasure. (Seriously, y'all are the best!)

In the words of brilliant creator Radha Blank: Find Your Own Vision.

CHAPTER 1

BROOKLYN, "THE BIG MISTAKE" AND VITAGRAPH STUDIOS

Brooklyn was a dream. All the things that happened there just couldn't happen. It was all dream stuff. Or was it all real and true, and was it that she, Francie, was the dreamer?
—*Betty Smith*, A Tree Grows in Brooklyn

Home to 2.5 million people (approximately the same size as Chicago), Brooklyn is the largest borough of New York City and known as the "fourth-largest city in America." On January 1, 1898, it was officially named part of the central city, and from then on, it lost its independence, becoming part of a considerable contingent of politicians.

"The Big Mistake" (as it became known) was a sore spot for several generations of Brooklynites, as this was home to some of the best America created, including teddy bears (dreamed up in honor of Theodore Roosevelt), roller coasters and hot dogs.

The Brooklyn Dodgers was the first professional baseball organization to sign an African American player to its team (Jackie Robinson in 1947), and the Flatbush National Bank of Brooklyn started a "Charge-It" program in 1946, which basically were the first credit cards produced. Benjamin Eisenstadt developed Sweet'N Low in 1957 after running a cafeteria at the Brooklyn Navy Yard when his wife complained about using a communal sugar jar at diners.

Brooklyn is also the birthplace of Mack Trucks, Brillo cleaning pads, Bazooka gum, Twizzlers and possibly the most significant contributor to comfort in the twentieth century—air conditioning. (Bushwick's Willis

Vitagraph founders, *left to right*: William T. "Pop" Rock, Albert E. Smith and James Stuart Blackton (1916). *From* The Movie Picture World *magazine.*

Carrier figured out how to eliminate humidity from a room in 1901, making the Sacket & Wilhelm's Printing Plant one of the best places to work in the summer months.)

It is also the location of one of the first movie studios globally: the Vitagraph Company formed in 1897 and lasted until 1925 with the advent of the "talkies," which started to take over the world as a top pastime.

In 1896, James Stuart Blackton (known as J. Stuart Blackton professionally), a *New York Evening World* reporter whose family originally made their way to Brooklyn from Yorkshire, England, interviewed famous inventor Thomas Edison to check out his newest creation: the Vitaphone, the first film projector.

Edison was never one to turn down an opportunity to see his name in print. He took Blackton to the cabin built specifically for creating these moving pictures in his New Jersey backyard. He could not have imagined that underneath the reporter's "just looking for a news story" veneer was a sharp businessman looking to make money in a fun and exciting industry with seemingly limitless growth. (He found the stage and theater world to be déclassé and wanted to reach paying customers outside New York City.)

Blackton took the invention back to New York City from Edison's lab and partnered with fellow Brit Albert E. Smith, a magician and actor who also fancied himself a director, to set up screenings of a new form of art— movies. Smith would play the Edison-created short films between his magic sets, and the audience attendance snowballed as the sight of pictures in motion thrilled people.

Vitagraph
Studios, 1911.
From The
Nickelodeon
magazine.

One year later (while both were in their early twenties), Blackton and Smith launched the American Vitagraph Company in downtown Manhattan before moving into a fully functioning movie studio built from the ground up in the Midwood section of Brooklyn, close to the elevated subway M line. At the time, the area was mainly farmland, with lovely homes lining the borough's shoreline for the wealthy to enjoy. Midwood was quiet compared to the noisy island of Manhattan, which quickly gained an immigrant population from all over the globe.

In 1905, the studio was built in what was initially known as Greenfield before being renamed Midwood. The land was so vast and quiet that the construction of a two-hundred-by-two-hundred-foot lot did not disturb the community. A diesel generator would help serve as a place to produce, shoot, write and edit films all in one location. Smith and Blackburn kept their offices on-site, and a chimney was replaced with a large smokestack with VITAGRAPH down one side, visible hundreds of feet away.

According to *Vitagraph: America's First Great Motion Picture Studio* by Andrew A. Erish, "Vitagraph encompasses the birth and development of motion pictures in America. The story's beginning follows the narrative of impoverished young immigrants who got off the boat with little more than a tentative drive to pursue the American Dream. It led them to an industry that hadn't yet been invented."

Most people who lived in Brooklyn at the time did so because they could afford it or just wanted to live off the land. Few *worked* in Brooklyn until Vitagraph started filming at its new studio. There were no bodegas or stores

Production still of *Lady Godiva* (1911), starring Kate Price (*left*) and Julia Swayne Gordon. *From* The Moving Picture World.

nearby. The top actors and talent lived in "the city" and would never think to take the subway (over one hundred feet in the air) out to the country comparatively.

Besides, motion pictures were quickly taking over as the lowest rung on the entertainment ladder. Unlike vaudeville comics, exotic dancers and magicians, *real* artists worked on a stage. After decades of theater people being considered degenerates on the outer edges of polite society, now they were regarded as top-tier entertainment.

People paid to see them live and in person. Movie acting, with the body and facial gestures that had to be broad (due to the lack of sound) and the entire story being told from start to finish in ten minutes, seemed both impersonal and a waste of money. According to the artistic elite, whatever Edison invented was crude and did not require actual skill.

But Blackton and Smith could picture a world where movies would get grander in scale and include a large cast, costumes, locations and (eventually) sound. To prove this, they took their cameras around the world. Vitagraph was on-site for the Spanish-American War of 1898 and created propaganda in motion pictures, including faking battle scenes with a brand-new stop-motion technique. Audiences were mesmerized by what they saw, and policies changed because politicians could see how passionate people became while watching news clips.

The newly created Midwood studio had space for gunfights, train derailments, bank robberies and romantic settings. Up-and-coming actors like Helen Hayes, Norma Talmadge and the first "Vitagraph Girl," Florence Turner, graced the screens and gained fans worldwide. A young Rudolph Valentino applied to be in the set creation department and quickly rose to lead actor on his way to international superstardom.

"The Vitagraph Girl," Florence Turner, 1912. *From Cinema News and Property Gazette.*

To bring these films to life meant dozens (and eventually hundreds) of workers who would manage the set, create costumes and props and serve as actors and extras. According to the *Brooklyn Daily Eagle* (1933), Vitagraph "also required of actors that they help in other directions, such as assisting to construct 'props' and scenery."

When filming *Romeo and Juliet* in 1900, according to *The Big V: A History of the Vitagraph Company* by Anthony Slide in 1987, the balcony scene was forgotten until the last minute. The actor who was playing Romeo had to build his own.

The actors and crew would arrive at first light and then close at sunset as electric lights and streetlamps were not yet a part of the neighborhood. There was also a need to bring food, as they were so far inland that there were no stores or restaurants. The solution for this was like many industries that relied on cheap, reliable labor—immigrants.

They arrived at Ellis Island seeking a better life for themselves and their families, taking whatever work they could get and trying to learn English as fast as they could. Most of Vitagraph's employees came from Manhattan's Lower East Side, Chinatown and Hell's Kitchen neighborhoods to take the M train to the studio.

The set was home to dozens of languages, which created a communication issue. The actors and crew learned foreign expressions and the occasional curse word from one another. Vitagraph was successful in silent films because so much pantomime was needed to communicate between people and departments. It did not feel silly to make exaggerated faces or gestures all day long, both on and off camera, to get through the day's work.

The workers were told which costumes and props were to be brought from home each week. Instructions such as "We are filming Dickens's *A Christmas Carol* so bring anything that looks British and at Christmas time" were given at the end of the shoot to prep for the following day. The need for new films (which at the time averaged fifteen to twenty minutes in length) caused the filmmakers to search for what we now call IP (intellectual property), and the first adaptations of Shakespeare, Dickens and Tolstoy were created at the Midwood studio.

After visiting the garment district to find scraps of fabric on the cheap, the families of the Vitagraph workers would create costumes and props and put them in large baskets. For five dollars per day, an employee could make a decent living and learn a trade while they helped pioneer a new form of entertainment. It is rumored that Leon Trotsky worked as an extra at Vitagraph.

Riding to Midwood, the train would stop at Avenue M, where men, women and children would cautiously walk down from the subway platform

Publicity still for Vitagraph "Fashion Reels for Women," 1913. *Courtesy of the Brooklyn Public Library.*

with their costumes and props in their baskets, filled to the brim with fake swords, hula skirts, cowboy gear, Santa suits, old-timey railroad uniforms and policeman outfits. If they were lucky, there would be enough room in storage to keep them overnight. Otherwise, many quickly learned the Yiddish word *schlep*, trudging back up the stairs to take the train home.

Blackton initially starred in and directed many films, creating the first animated movies in film history. His hand drawings came to life in 1899 with the silent short *The Enchanted Drawing* (the first 35 mm animated film), and he went on to create dozens more over the next decade, influencing generations of filmmakers to come.

In 1915, Blackton was passionate about America's cause to join the Allies in World War I. He produced the propaganda film *The Battle Cry of Peace* with the support and blessing of former president Theodore Roosevelt. At the time, the press compared it in intensity with the newly released *The Birth of a Nation*.

Vitagraph also had the first movie stars who gained international fame, including comedic actor John Bunny, whose death in 1915 made worldwide news years before Charlie Chaplin. Service members collected postcards of Vitagraph Girls during World War I. The studio had its problems with more than one enthusiastic actor/comedian who dreamed of being a star and stalked the Midwood offices, including Moe Howard, who would later find success with the Three Stooges.

According to the *Brooklyn Daily Eagle* (1933), the Vitagraph Company was created without a written agreement between Blackton, Smith and William "Pop" Rock (Vitagraph's first president), and "by 1912 [they] were dividing profits of $5–6 million" (the equivalent of $200 million in today's dollars). Rock was called "Pop" because he was several decades older than the founders of Vitagraph. He was responsible for acquiring films around the globe to add to their stock, including early boxing footage of champion Jack Johnson.

In 1925, Smith sold the studio to Warner Brothers for $1 million (the equivalent of $15 million today) and retired in Hollywood. In 1948, he received an Academy Award for being "one of the small group of pioneers who believed in a new medium." He died on August 1, 1958.

His former partner Blackton (who lost his fortune in the stock market crash of 1929) spent the rest of his life showing Vitagraph silent movies in lectures around the country. He died after being hit by a car in 1941. At the time, he was working with Hal Roach on developing color films.

Battle scene Vitagraph, 1915. *Library of Congress.*

Vitagraph Camp, Commodore J. Stuart Blackton, 1915. *Library of Congress.*

Vitagraph smokestack, 1277 East 15th Street (Midwood), November 2021.

For years, the Midwood studios were the location for early sound pictures and the starting place for various actors, including Humphrey Bogart, Jack Benny, Spencer Tracy, Sammy Davis Jr. and Cyd Charisse.

The building was sold in 1965 to the Shulamith School for Girls (which was ironic considering the men who designed and created the buildings were anti-Semitic), with the original smokestack still in place. The Vitagraph smokestack is visible from the subway as the riders of the elevated M train go by that stop and was never taken down, despite changing ownership over the years. It is the last visible reminder of Vitagraph studios.

In 2012, the Landmarks Preservation Commission of Brooklyn did not think the structure contained any "architectural merit" and initially planned to allow it to be torn down by the new owners to build a new residential apartment complex. Fortunately, the Vitagraph apartments in Midwood have used the landmark as part of their total design concept, and it still stands in place today.

Located at 1277 East 14th Street (by Avenue M), you can still find the original site from the Long Island Railroad.

CHAPTER 2

BROWNSTONE BROOKLYN

In Park Slope, even the Play Do is whole grain.
—author Sarah Pinneo

Among the most iconic images of Brooklyn are those of the brownstones found throughout the borough. These townhouses rose in popularity in the late nineteenth century and early part of the twentieth and were named for the brown sandstone that became a popular building material across the United States. They are found throughout New York City, with clusters in Brooklyn in Bedford Stuyvesant, Park Slope, Carroll Gardens, Cobble Hill, Windsor Terrace, Clinton Hill, Crown Heights, Williamsburg, Brooklyn Heights, Bay Ridge and Sunset Park.

The homes were large enough to hold several generations of families and rent out for boarders and were often designed with a large set of stairs on the entryway called a "stoop." Trust that "stoop life" is everything when you live in a brownstone. It's where you sit and have coffee in the morning; it's where you hang out to catch a summer breeze; it is a designated "chill zone" where conversation flows and New Yorkers find it in themselves to hang out, slow down and take a break. If you have kids, this is where they take colored pieces of chalk to draw and play hopscotch. It's the perfect spot to sit on a first date and see how things are going. It is the best place to hang out and gossip about the neighborhood.

In the 1950s and '60s, the crime rate began to rise so high that people started to decamp to the suburbs in Staten Island, Long Island, Westchester

3rd Street between 7th and 8th Avenue, (Park Slope), April 2021.

and New Jersey. City living was no longer considered calm or safe. New York City was so broke that garbage strikes were frequent, and the police often threatened to strike.

From 1976 to 1977, New York endured a serial killer who targeted couples and women for fourteen months using a .44-caliber pistol. (The "Son of Sam," David Berkowitz, was captured in 1977 and has been in prison ever since.)

On July 13, 1977, a blackout hit New York City that lasted for twenty-five hours and threw the city into chaos.

Many films show New York City in the '60s, '70s and '80s reflecting a tough, grimy place where danger was rampant and the city's future was in question. *Saturday Night Fever, Taxi Driver* and *The French Connection* reflect this "urban life is becoming a nightmare" trend.

A funny thing began happening in the '80s. Large brownstones were left behind in disrepair. Entire neighborhoods became vacated, and four-story homes were selling for $25,000 (or less!). Artists, teachers and young professionals sought to live the city life that included a backyard or at least close access to parks, as well as buildings and neighborhoods that had over a century of history to them. This may sound like no big deal to any Europeans doing this, but America is a ridiculously young country; some might say that is part of our charm!

These days, the price of the average home in Park Slope alone is $1.2 million, and it is considered a status symbol to be able to afford a brownstone. Much of this can be attributed to the crime rate dropping by 81 percent since 1990.

Brooklyn has a thriving tech economy and a vast community of artists and makers, which helps with the image of Brooklyn as a new Bohemia. It's a land with history but is always facing the future. It's organic, breathing and full of life.

When I first moved to Park Slope, I would stroll around the streets and avenues woozy from enchantment. It's no surprise filmmakers have used it and several other neighborhoods in Brooklyn as part of the character and tone of their stories.

The Amazing Spider-Man home, 36 Fuller Place (Windsor Terrace), 2021.

The Amazing Spider-Man (2012)

The 2012 version of Spider-Man had Andrew Garfield playing the teen superhero but sticks with the basics of most of Spidey's story. Peter Parker is raised by Uncle Ben and Aunt May in New York City and is an undercover fighter of villains (including Rhys Ifans as "The Lizard") after school and at night. The Parker home is nestled on a lovely street in Windsor Terrace.

Anchorman 2: The Legend Continues (2013)

Between 7th and 8th Avenues in Park Slope is an often-used film and TV shooting location with more *Law & Order* (and their variants) episodes than can be tallied in one book. In the photo here, you see the spot where we first find Christina Applegate's character in *Anchorman 2: The Legend Continues*. Ron Burgundy (Will Farrell) comes to New York to try his hand at cable TV news and win back Applegate's Veronica Corningstone, who has settled

The block where Veronica Corningstone (Christina Applegate) lives in *Anchorman 2: The Legend Continues*, 3rd Street (Park Slope), April 2021.

into life as a brownstone dweller. Farrell's visit to 3rd Street brought *Anchorman* fans from all over the city.

Eat Pray Love (2010)

The *Eat Pray Love* home, 172 Pacific Street (Cobble Hill), September 2021.

Eat Pray Love, directed by Ryan Murphy and starring Julia Roberts, is an adaptation of the smash hit autobiography by writer Elizabeth Gilbert, who journeyed through Italy, India and Indonesia to recover from a breakup. The movie begins "Liz Gilbert's" journey in Carroll Gardens and Clinton Hill's neighborhoods with Roberts visiting the revered (and much missed) bookstore BookCourt and hosting a chic cocktail party at home with her husband, Stephen (Billy Crudup), before their split.

The carriage house (at 172 Pacific Street) made headlines when it was sold for over $6 million to singer/songwriter Norah Jones in 2015. The streets surrounding make for a perfect afternoon of walking and shopping.

> *In full transparency, I will admit that I am an unabashed fan and devotee of Elizabeth Gilbert. Her work has profoundly impacted how I view and manifest my journey in creative living. Although* Eat Pray Love *was Gilbert's breakout work, it was work she was writing for herself. She was on a journey, and the trinity arc of the development is wholly specific to her. But that is the magic of the work—so many people talk with her about the part in the book where "XYZ changed my life." Elizabeth Gilbert will tell you that "XYZ" is nowhere in the book. It is a work that people will take and fold into themselves in very personal ways that often exist nowhere in the narrative.*
>
> *Naturally, I was curious about how this film—with Julia Roberts in place of Elizabeth Gilbert—would translate into film. I did not need to worry—it is a film about change, discovery, faith and wonder. I will gladly watch this adaptation any old time. It is a balm of sorts; I will always find the thread I need for a little extra wisdom and grace.*
>
> —*Alicia Mintz, co-creator and host of* Trashy Divorces *podcast*

The Intern (2015)

Anne Hathaway in *The Intern* (2015) has a swoon-worthy kitchen, an adorable family and a brownstone based in trendy Clinton Hill. She is also the CEO of a giant tech company whose life is falling apart.

Hathaway hires a seventy-year-old retiree as her intern (played by Robert DeNiro), who helps her with her business and (surprise!) her relationships. Several outdoor shots were filmed in Carroll Gardens on Cheever Place, and if you are in Williamsburg, you will find Teddy's Bar & Grill (96 Berry Street), where Hathaway's character imbibes too much. To achieve a perfect Nancy Meyers heroine look, wear an all-white outfit, high heels and shiny hair.

The Intern brownstone, 383 Grand Street (Clinton Hill), July 2021.

Motherless Brooklyn (2019)

Edward Norton's directorial debut is an adaptation of Jonathan Lethem's bestselling novel and filmed throughout Bedford Stuyvesant and Fort Greene. It transforms an entire block in Brooklyn Heights (Henry Street between Orange and Pineapple Streets) to create the look of 1950s New York City. Costars include Alec Baldwin, Gugu Mbatha-Raw and Willem Dafoe.

Norton plays Lionel Essrog, a lonely private detective with Tourette's syndrome trying to solve the murder of his only friend. The actor/director, a Baltimore native, moved to New York in 1991 and is a huge booster of the city, as he told Bloomberg News in 2019. He said working with director Spike Lee on *25th Hour* motivated him to try to shoot a period piece. "I really learned from Spike more than anyone else." About the film's dark undertones, he said, "In many ways, even though it's a movie about tough things and happened in New York, it's reflective of my love affair with the city."

The Sentinel (1977)

This 1977 horror film directed by Michael Winner (*Deathwish*) has everything a cheesy scary flick needs to tell a story of nefarious spirits threatening to take over the world. A beautiful actress (Christina Raines) plays a model who moves into a Brooklyn Heights brownstone with a dark past possessed by evil spirits. For $400 a month (!), she rents a fully furnished apartment that features a blind nun who watches from the highest-floor window (our sentinel). It also stars Jeff Goldblum, Jerry Orbach, Beverly D'Angelo, Christopher Sarandon, Ava Gardner, Christopher Walken, Tom Berenger and Burgess Meredith.

> The Sentinel *shows a dream New York…that quickly devolves into Hell. A beautiful brownstone becomes the doorway into a dimension of murders and mayhem—and only the chosen can keep the door shut.*
> —*Robyn Buckley of* F This Movie! *podcast*

The Sentinel corner, 10 Montague Street (Brooklyn Heights), June 2021.

The home located at 10 Montague Terrace was built in 1875 and features fantastic views of Manhattan and lovely tree-lined streets. Once owned by the Sanger family (considered the elite in Brooklyn society), the building was passed down to family members until the 1950s, when Brooklyn Heights seemed neglectful. It is now the home to several families, and even after the construction of the Brooklyn Queens Expressway, it has some of the most spectacular views of the city.

FYI, 8 Montague Terrace set the record in January 2021 for being the most expensive property sold in Brooklyn at $25 million by Vincent Viola, the owner of the Florida Panthers hockey team.

Sophie's Choice (1982)

Ditmas Park offers a mid-twentieth-century American vibe with its stately homes, wraparound porches and manicured lawns galore. It was the perfect setting for 1982's *Sophie's Choice*, directed by Alan J. Pakula (*All the President's Men, The Pelican Brief*) and based on the novel by William Styron. It stars Meryl Streep in an Academy Award–winning performance as the lead character Sophie. This woman survived the Nazis and a concentration

Sophie's Choice home, 101 Rugby Street (Ditmas Park), May 2021.

camp by making the most horrible decision anyone would have to make. (I won't give it away, but the expression "making a Sophie's Choice" is rarely a wise or thoughtful choice of words.)

Pakula told the *New York Times* in 1982, "It's a classic loss of innocence story, a classic rite of passage. There's the complexity of the relationships between Nathan and Sophie, as seen through the young man's eyes. There's the strange mixture of life-giving and death-giving in the relationship, the ambivalence of love carried to its most intense extreme."

It co-stars Kevin Kline as her lover Nathan and Peter MacNicol as their neighbor Stingo, who accompanies them on a trip to Coney Island. Generally, Stingo is the happy third wheel in their relationship. The actual home used was painted pink to reflect the setting of post–World War II America and can be found at 101 Rugby Road. (You will want to walk around to enjoy the entire neighborhood for the afternoon!)

War of the Worlds (2005)

Park Slope in place of Boston for *War of the Worlds*, 787 Carroll Street, June 2021.

Steven Spielberg's adaptation on the classic H.G. Wells novel stars Tom Cruise as Ray Ferrier from Bayonne, New Jersey, who is escaping an alien invasion with his children to bring them safely to their grandmother's home in Boston. Park Slope's Carrol Street between 8th Avenue and Prospect Park West is the "Boston" setting for the last scene depicting the grandparents (played by the stars of the 1953 original film, Ann Robinson and Gene Barry) welcoming their granddaughter (Dakota Fanning). This location has been used in many films and TV productions for its gorgeous scenery.

More brownstones can be found in chapter 9 with our movie listings by neighborhood.

CHAPTER 3

THE BROOKLYN BRIDGE AND THE BROOKLYN HEIGHTS PROMENADE

You have waited, you always wait, you dumb, beautiful ministers,
We receive you with free sense at last, and are instantiate henceforward,
Not you any more shall be able to foil us, or withhold yourselves from us,
We use you, and do not cast you aside—we plant you permanently with us,
We fathom you not—we love you—there is perfection in you also,
You furnish your parts toward eternity,
Great or small, you furnish your parts toward the soul
—Walt Whitman, "Crossing Brooklyn Ferry" (1856)

I'd rather be the man who bought the Brooklyn Bridge than the man who sold it.
—Will Rogers (1879–1935)

There are two enduring symbols and experiences of Brooklyn featured perennially in books, television and movies for over one hundred years. The Brooklyn Bridge and the Brooklyn Promenade walkway (also known as the Esplanade) have become symbols of man's ingenuity. The Brooklyn Bridge was the largest suspension bridge when it was opened to the public in 1883, and the beauty lies in urban structures next to nature.

Emily Warren Roebling taught herself engineering to help complete her husband and father-in-law's work (John and Washington Roebling) when they succumbed to various illnesses during the bridge's construction. It is the destination for millions every day who are either looking toward "the city" or "going home" to Brooklyn.

Top: Will Smith, *I Am Legend*, 2007. *AA Film Archive/Alamy Stock Photo*.

Bottom: Diane Keaton and Woody Allen, *Annie Hall*, 1977. *APL Archive/Alamy Stock Photo*.

By connecting Manhattan and Brooklyn, a greater New York City idea began in 1897, when Brooklyn was the fourth-most populated city in the United States. For many Brooklynites, joining New York as a borough along with Manhattan, Bronx, Queens and Staten Island made Brooklyn inferior and kept it "lesser than" Manhattan.

There are other bridges and tunnels built to connect all the boroughs. Still, there is nothing quite like the original Brooklyn Bridge to symbolize the manufactured structures that fulfill a basic need and are also so achingly beautiful. It is very New York, very American and a crowning jewel of the borough for its residents.

The area of the Promenade is a platform over the Brooklyn-Queens Expressway and was created to connect the boroughs while keeping the aesthetic of New York City's horizon. Originally, it was lined with warehouses, but when New York City parks commissioner Robert Moses (a controversial figure in the city) planned to bisect Brooklyn Heights with the future expressway in 1943, the community rallied to preserve the area and view.

The Promenade was opened to the public in 1950. At over 1,800 feet in length and having spectacular views, the site has been used in movies for decades, including *Annie Hall*, *Moonstruck*, *Spider-Man 2*, *Saturday Night Fever* and *Remember Me*.

In some instances, the Brooklyn Bridge symbolizes the quintessential New York City visitor's experience, with the Manhattan skyline prominently in the background and an air of fun and lightheartedness. Actor Seann William Scott tweeted, "Everyone should walk across the Brooklyn Bridge. I did it three times in a row because it was one of the most exhilarating experiences I've ever had. The view is breathtaking."

For several years in the 1980s and 1990s, Brooklyn native Jerry Seinfeld would walk across the bridge on New Year's Day as a tradition with comedy pals Paul Reiser and Larry Miller.

Enchanted (2007)

In *Enchanted*, Amy Adams is Giselle, a woman from another land sent by an evil queen (Susan Sarandon) to New York City to avoid marrying her stepson, Prince Edward. Giselle falls in love with an attorney (Patrick Dempsey), who then tells her she should marry the prince and move back to her natural home. Giselle and Edward spend the day in New York, culminating in a trip over the Brooklyn Bridge as the ultimate tourist destination. (Spoiler—she stays with the Dempsey character, and they live happily ever after!) Adams recently filmed the sequel and promised the story (and her character) would go off in an exciting direction.

Brooklyn Bridge arch, July 2021.

THE BRIDGE CAN BE a place of excitement and uncertainty, with chase scenes like in *Godzilla*, *The French Connection* and *Fantastic Four*. Watching a site where millions travel back and forth, the action is interrupted by (fictional) mass destruction, as we see in *The Day After Tomorrow*, *Deep Impact* and *Cloverfield*. The symbol of the bridge being destroyed means a part of America is harmed as well.

"Ho Volgia di te" (2007)

2007's Italian film *"Ho Volgia di te"* in English means "I Want You" and features two characters who cement their true love by attaching a lock to a bridge. Since then, thousands of people worldwide have attached locks to bridges, including the Brooklyn Bridge. It is not encouraged (really, the people who must cut those locks off on the regular would *really* like this trend to end!) but is a thing that happens.

Left: Brooklyn Bridge with locks, July 2021.

Right: Brooklyn Bridge with signs from visitors, July 2021.

I Am Legend (2007)

Will Smith deals with the end of the world (via a world plague) with a trusty dog (don't get too attached to him!) while fighting mutants around New York City. The Richard Matheson novel is considered a sci-fi classic, and the film's visuals of a dilapidated city are genuinely memorable.

Kate & Leopold (2001)

In the movie *Kate & Leopold*, the Brooklyn Bridge serves as a portal for the character of Leopold (His Grace, Third Duke of Albany), played by Hugh Jackman, a nobleman of Brooklyn in 1876. He inadvertently uses the Brooklyn Bridge, which is not yet completed, as a time portal to modern-day New York City in 2001. Others on this wacky adventure include Liev Schreiber, Breckin Meyer and Natasha Lyonne. Does he find love with modern-day Kate, played by Meg Ryan? (Do you *not* know your chick flicks, people!)

MARVEL FILMS

The bridge holds a special place for Peter Parker (aka Spider-Man) in almost all the Marvel films of the last twenty years. Peter is a teenager in New York City, and at times he needs to fight a foe on the Brooklyn Bridge to save Mary Jane (Kirsten Dunst), as he does in the film *Spider-Man 2* (2004). In *Fantastic Four* (the 2005 version), Jessica Alba as Sue Storm is stripped down to her underwear on the bridge for some important reason.

Mo' Better Blues (1990)

The bridge can also symbolize loneliness, as with Denzel Washington's character in Spike Lee's *Mo' Better Blues*, in which he depicts musician Bleek Gilliam playing saxophone by himself into the night. The audience for jazz is getting smaller, but he can still find a spot in New York City to perform. This film also stars Lee, Wesley Snipes, Giancarlo Esposito, Joie Lee and Robin Harris.

Sex and the City: The Movie (2008)

The first big-screen adaptation of the cherished series (1998–2004) features a significant plotline about the marriage of Miranda Hobbes (Cynthia Nixon) and Steve Brady (David Eigenberg), who have broken up partly over her anger at him "making" her move to Brooklyn. He finally gives her an ultimatum: meet me at the Brooklyn Bridge or let us break up forever. (Spoiler—they reunite!)

The HBO update ...*And Just Like That* has fans up in arms over the treatment of Steve and Miranda's fading affection for him. But we will always have the 2008 film and the gorgeous bridge scene to remind us of their love that was real and enduring.

> *What a film! Although the television series did an incredible job of showing off New York City, this film was something else! The backdrop of New York City is the uncredited yet fully present extra character in the film. I had not traveled to NYC until after the film's release. I did get there in the winter of 2009, and it was one of the oddest feelings I have ever experienced. It was a déjà vu in the fullest sense. In a car driving over the Brooklyn Bridge on a rainy afternoon, I had this feeling that I had never felt more at home exactly where I was. There was a familiarity everywhere—the streets, the architecture, the people. I have no explanation for this strange and wonderful feeling other than the dedication of filmmakers paying homage to the greatest city in the world.*
> —*Alicia Mintz, co-creator and host of* Trashy Divorces *podcast*

The Siege (1998)

In this Bruce Willis and Denzel Washington film, a wave of terrorism throughout New York City causes martial law to be declared, which means a scene with U.S. tanks taking over the Brooklyn Bridge. The message is, if you want to take over New York, we will fight you at our most cherished monument. (Much jingoism here!) Rounding out the cast are Annette Bening, Tony Shalhoub and Lance Reddick.

The Wedding Banquet (1993)

Director Ang Lee's Asian American comedy is about a gay man (Winston Chao) who marries a Chinese woman (Mary Chin) to give her citizenship. This also stops his family from asking questions about his love life while he decides how to live his most honest existence. A pivotal scene takes place on the Brooklyn Bridge and changes the story's trajectory. (I will not spoil that detail!)

Brooklyn Promenade in the light, May 2021.

When I saw The Wedding Banquet *(1993) as a teenager, I couldn't help but smile through the entire film—not just because it is a delightfully written and directed romantic comedy. It was, at the time, the first movie I'd ever seen set in Brooklyn starring people who looked like me. It was also one of the first movies centered around gay characters in the theater. It's now nearly thirty years later, and sadly, it's still one of the only films I can think of that checks both of those boxes. You'd think we would have come along further by now!*

—*Kristen Meinzer, co-host of* By the Book *and* Movie Therapy with Rafer & Kristen *and culture critic*

The Brooklyn Promenade is an 1,826-foot (557-meter) platform that runs outside Brooklyn Heights and the Brooklyn Queens Expressway. It gives a fantastic view of Manhattan and being pedestrian-only makes it an excellent location to film characters meditating on life (such as in *Spider-Man* and *John Wick*). Or, as in *Annie Hall*, it is the perfect spot for lovers where the two leads declare their "like" for one another.

THE FOLLOWING IS BY no means a complete list of films on (or near) the bridge or the Promenade, giving an idea of the variety of stories they tell visually.

- *The Angriest Man in Brooklyn* (2014) One of the final on-screen performances by Robin Williams, with Mila Kunis, Peter Dinklage and Richard Kind.
- *Annie Hall* (1977) Woody Allen's classic meditation on love with Diane Keaton.
- *Black Rain* (1989) A 1980s action thriller with Michael Douglas in a mullet and Andy Garcia looking very fine.
- *Click* (2006) Adam Sandler has a "universal remote" that can "fast forward" and "skip" his real life. With Kate Beckinsale, Christopher Walken and David Hasselhoff.
- *Cloverfield* (2008) Jiggly camera work and scary monsters invade New York to scare Lizzy Caplan, Mike Vogel and Jessica Lucas.
- *C'mon C'mon* (2021) Joaquin Phoenix travels across the country with his nephew, played by Woody Norman.
- *The Day After Tomorrow* (2004) The world is frozen over, with Dennis Quaid and Jake Gyllenhaal as the main heroes.
- *Death Wish* (1974) Charles Bronson is mad as hell and not taking it anymore. With Hope Lange, Vincent Gardenia and Jeff Goldblum.
- *Deep Impact* (1998) New York City is blown up with an asteroid. With Téa Leoni.
- *Donnie Brasco* (1997) Al Pacino and Johnny Depp are a mobster and an FBI agent in gritty New York City.
- *Enchanted* (2007) Amy Adams is a real-life princess trying to find love in the "real world." She takes Prince Edward (a super funny James Marsden) for a stroll on the bridge.
- *Fantastic Four* (2005) A Marvel film with Chris Evans as Johnny Storm, Ioan Gruffudd as Reed Richards and Michael Chiklis as Ben Grimm.
- *The French Connection* (1971) William Friedkin did not get permits to film on the bridge, supposedly. (He tells a lot of tall tales, by the way.)
- *Friends with Kids* (2011) Two best friends (played by Jennifer Westfeldt and Adam Scott) decide to have a kid but not be together romantically.
- *Godzilla* (1998) A big lizard attacks New York City against a befuddled Matthew Broderick.
- *A Hatful of Rain* (1957) A Marine veteran (Don Murray) deals with drug addiction.

Brooklyn Bridge heading toward Manhattan, July 2021.

- *House of D* (2004) David Duchovny wrote and directed this drama about an artist with a troubled past, starring Téa Leoni and Robin Williams.
- *Hudson Hawk* (1991) Bruce Willis and Danny Aiello add to the popular "caper/musical" genre. You either love or loathe this film.
- *I Am Legend* (2007) Will Smith battles monsters who take over New York after a plague.
- *Inside Man* (2006) Spike Lee directs this tight thriller with Denzel Washington and Jodie Foster about a bank heist (or is it?).
- *In the Cut* (2003) A sexy drama starring Meg Ryan, who wanted to ditch the "America's sweetheart" image with this Jane Champion production. With Mark Ruffalo and Jennifer Jason Leigh.
- *It Happened in Brooklyn* (1947) Frank Sinatra is an army guy who misses Brooklyn.
- *John Wick: Chapter 2* (2014) Keanu Reeves being sexy and fighting people is always a winning combo.
- *Kate & Leopold* (2001) Hugh Jackman transports through time in the most bizarre time machine ever.

- *The Kitchen* (2019) A period piece (the 1970s) with Melissa McCarthy and Tiffany Haddish about gangsters who run their husbands' rackets after they are sent to prison.
- *Limitless* (2011) Bradley Cooper takes a pill and becomes a financial genius. With Robert DeNiro.
- *Manhattan* (1979) Woody Allen's classic with a "this is really who I am!" message. He plays a forty-year-old who woos a teenager (Mariel Hemingway). Also stars Diane Keaton, Meryl Streep and Wallace Shawn.
- *Marathon Man* (1976) Dustin Hoffman is being chased by Nazis who use dental equipment.
- *Mo' Better Blues* (1990) Denzel Washington is a lover and jazz musician.
- *Mr. & Mrs. Smith* (2005) Brad Pitt and Angelina Jolie are married, and they each find out the other is a spy. It's silly, but they are hot and watchable.
- *'neath Brooklyn Bridge* (1942) The East Side Kids adventure, now in the public domain.
- *Nerve* (2016) Emma Roberts and Dave Franco star in this all-over-the-place (not in a good way) thriller.
- *Newsies* (1992) Technically not on the bridge, but the special effects make it look like the real thing, and most of my friends love this film. With Christian Bale, Robert Duvall and Ann-Margret.
- *Night on Earth* (1991) A Jim Jarmusch film about cab drivers around the world, including Winona Ryder, Giancarlo Esposito and Rosie Perez.
- *Now You See Me* (2013) Illusionists pull off heists around New York. With Jesse Eisenberg, Common, Mark Ruffalo and Woody Harrelson.
- *Oliver & Company* (1988) This is an animated film with Billy Joel and Joey Lawrence, with a Brooklyn Bridge scene that is completely adorable.
- *On the Town* (1949) Gene Kelly and Frank Sinatra sing and dance around New York in this classic musical.
- *Over the Brooklyn Bridge* (1984) Elliott Gould is a Brooklyn boy ready to move to Manhattan. Features an impressive "walk over the Brooklyn Bridge" scene.

- *Remember Me* (2010) A 9/11 romance with Robert Pattinson.
- *St. Vincent* (2014) Melissa McCarthy and Bill Murray star in this indie comedy about next-door neighbors.
- *Saturday Night Fever* (1977) John Travolta dreams about moving to "the city" and leaving Bay Ridge behind.
- *Sex and the City: The Movie* (2008) "Miranda and Steve" totally get back together in this film, and I will accept no other narrative.
- *The Siege* (1998) Terrorists take over New York. With Bruce Willis.
- *Smoke* (1995) Harvey Keitel and Stockard Channing walk along the Promenade.
- *Sophie's Choice* (1982) Post–World War II movie with Meryl Streep and Kevin Kline that is very intense.
- *Spider-Man* (2002) Tobey Maguire as the hero with web powers.
- *Spider-Man: Homecoming* (2014) Andrew Garfield as the second hero teen in tights.
- *Stay* (2005) A psychological thriller with Ewan McGregor and Naomi Watts.
- *Sweet November* (1968) Sandy Dennis plays a dying woman who dates men for exactly one month before dumping them. Seriously.

Brooklyn Promenade in the summer, July 2021.

- *Tarzan's New York Adventure* (1942) Tarzan takes his loincloth to New York.
- *Three Days of the Condor* (1975) A spy thriller with Robert Redford that is entirely great and thrilling.
- *Uncertainty* (2008) Joseph Gordon-Levitt's life changes because of a coin toss.
- *The Wedding Banquet* (1993) A Chinese American romance with a critical scene on the Brooklynn Bridge.
- *Wolfen* (1981) People are being killed around New York by other people with a "wolf spirit." Stars Albert Finney, Gregory Hines, Diane Venora and Edward James Olmos.

CHAPTER 4

CONEY ISLAND, BABY!

It is blatant; It is cheap.
It is the Apotheosis of the ridiculous
But it is something more
It is Niagara Falls
Or the Grand Canyon
Or Yellowstone Park
It is a National Playground
And not to have seen it
Is not to have seen your own country
—Reginald Wright Kauffman (1909)

Coney Island is as big of a symbol of New York City as it is about America itself. It is a place where the best and worst of our culture are celebrated with our love of the beach, amusement parks, thrilling roller coasters and hot dogs mixed with a grimy, barely under the surface malevolence. It's a place to relax and yet also be on your guard. To take in the beauty of the ocean while seeing remnants of its "freak show" past. To feel at ease and yet slightly on edge. Will it feel like you are in the middle of a Woody Allen film or *The Warriors*?

It began as a sleepy section of the beach at the farthest end of Brooklyn. The "conies" were the name of the wild rabbits that inhabited the land for two hundred years before someone thought the region might be suitable for docking boats that could not make it to the other harbors around New York City.

Above: Coney Island at dusk, July 2021.

Opposite: Elephant Colossus Hotel, Surf Avenue and West 12th Street, 1895 or 1896. *Wikimedia*.

Paddlewheel ships would dock, and there was food and drink, lodging, gambling and whatever else your heart desired and could afford. You could enjoy the sounds of seagulls flying around while trying to avoid pickpockets or the calls of a lady of the night to keep you company. It was not unusual for bodies to wash up on the shoreline on the island's western end.

On the eastern end was a pier and a sophisticated crowd of people enjoying nature as a respite from the rapidly growing city. The Industrial Revolution led to thousands of immigrants moving to the town to build skyscrapers, work in retail and perform whatever cheap labor was needed. People sought nature to divert from the concrete jungle, and Coney Island meant sun, sand and fun. In the mid-1800s, bathing suits came into fashion as a way for people to enjoy the water and maintain their modesty.

Coney Island soon became an incredible amalgam of modern machinery with its light display from Thomas Edison, rides like the Steeplechase and a 122-foot-high hotel shaped like an elephant, along with the carnival barkers and circus sideshow entertainment.

The smell of salt water in the air was also a considerable relief from the hot and muggy summers famous on the East Coast. When temperatures and humidity rose, there was no air conditioning to take refuge in for most homes and apartments. Going to Coney Island for the day (or a weekend) meant a respite from a fast-paced world, and "red hots" (now known as hot dogs) were a snack you could take on a stroll.

In the early 1900s, Brooklyn's Vitagraph and other emerging movie studios filmed on location at Coney Island to satisfy the need from viewers around the globe for the wanderlust to see New York and people on vacation (a new concept at the time.)

As the world changed, so did Coney Island.

In films, you can get a feel for the United States from how they film a scene set on Coney Island. From the rough-and-tumble early twentieth century to the more family-friendly 1930s–1950s to the racial issues of post–World War II America (mostly "white flight," where millions of white New Yorkers started to leave Brooklyn for the suburbs) into the 1970s, Coney Island speaks to the state of the United States and its people.

Coney Island was wholly burned down by the big fire of 1911 (turns out a place full of wood, tar and the early vestiges of electricity was a toxic combination) and then almost swept away by Hurricane Sandy in 2012. Every June, you can still enjoy a hot dog at Nathan's while viewing the Mermaid Parade.

It is a place that held onto its "freak shows" far longer than the politically correct world would deem acceptable, and it represents the hopes of people looking for a respite from a dizzying modern world.

Coney Island exists despite itself. It is old and skeevy, young and hopeful, tacky and classic at the same time. You can take F and Q trains out to the boardwalk anytime to see it for yourself.

Some of the most memorable movies that take place on Coney Island include:

Beaches (1988)

The story of C.C. Bloom (Bette Midler) and Hillary Whitney (Barbara Hershey) is one of the most beloved "chick flicks" of all time, with their friendship beginning under the piers of the Atlantic City boardwalk. Coney Island was the stand-in location, and it was a set filled with Brooklyn talent behind the scenes, who told me on Facebook they thoroughly enjoyed the experience.

Brooklyn (2015)

Emory Cohen as "Tony" and Saoirse Ronan as "Eilis" in *Brooklyn* (2015). *Twentieth Century Fox Film Corporation/ Picturelux/Alamy Stock Photo.*

Set in the 1950s, Irish immigrant Eilis Lacey (Brooklyn native Saoirse Ronan) spends a year in Brooklyn, where she falls in love with an Italian American. The beach scenes are filmed at the Coney Island boardwalk, where she learns how to dress/undress quickly on the beach. (Hint, wear a bathing suit as underwear!) Based on a novel by Colm Tóibín and screenplay by Nick Hornby, the John Crowley–directed film tells the story of Eilis, who leaves County Wexford in

Ireland and finds love and fulfillment in New York with *The Marvelous Mrs. Maisel* actor Michael Zegen. When an unexpected tragedy sends her back to her homeland, she must decide between a life of known comfort and one with an unpredictable future.

Requiem for a Dream (2000)

Director Darren Aronofsky adapted the novel from fellow Brooklynite Hubert Selby Jr. It is a tale of four people in Coney Island and their drug addictions. Ellen Burstyn was nominated for an Academy Award for her performance as Jared Leto's mother, who struggles with the ravages of aging and her dependence on diet pills.

The Warriors (1979)

The Warriors (1979), director Walter Hill. *Photo 12/Alamy Stock Photo.*

The cult classic from director Walter Hill is the tale of the Warriors gang of Coney Island being chased by an array of thugs, hoodlums and fighters over one night, including the Riffs, the Baseball Furies and the Lizzies. The Warriors try to make it home after being framed for the murder of one of the most feared gang leaders in New York (Cyrus, in a bravura performance by Roger Hill); they must fight their way through every gang territory between the Bronx and Brooklyn. It is led by Michael Beck, James Remar and Deborah Van Valkenburgh.

Filmed in the summer of 1978 on location, it shows New York City in the throes of its dark years, with garbage-filled streets and graffiti-filled subway cars. Eventually, they reach the Coney Island boardwalk, with an infamous scene of actor David Patrick Kelly clinking two glass bottles together and saying, "Warriors! Come out and play!" (Apparently, he improvised that on the spot during filming.)

In the end, the Warriors walk into the sunset as the Eagles' "In the City" blares over the closing credits. The real killer of Cyrus is being dealt with

Coney Island Boardwalk at dusk, August 2021.

"street justice" style, and the gang lives to see another day, wiser and more grateful for one another after a wild night.

Almost everything I know about New York, I learned from the movies. Movies have always been my Big Apple education, from Scorsese to Spike, from Lustig to Henenlotter. One of my favorite N.Y. movies has always been Walter Hill's The Warriors, *the cult classic about a street gang forced to travel from the Bronx to their home turf on Coney Island when they're framed for a murder.*

The way it turns the city into a danger zone was very much in keeping with the cinematic depictions of New York in the late 1970s and early '80s. Still, there was something so specific about the way The Warriors *turned every piece of New York—Riverside Park, the subway, you name it—into some ominous obstacle to be defeated, an urban jungle with danger lurking around every corner, that makes the movie stand out even among New York movies.*

Walter Hill made being in a gang like the Lizzies or the Baseball Furies look cool (hell, he even made Michael Beck look cool!). He turned The Warriors *into a travelogue of New York after dark, with only the voice of DJ Lynne Thigpen to guide you home to safety. When my wife and I*

The Warriors location on the beach, July 2021.

Coney Island beach at dusk, July 2021.

recently took a trip out to Brooklyn, we made sure to go out to Coney Island to pay tribute to The Warriors. *There wasn't a leather vest in sight, but I could still feel their presence.*

—*Patrick Bromley, host of the* F This Movie! *podcast and editor-in-chief of fthismovie.com*

CONEY ISLAND BOARDWALK IN PERIOD FILMS

The Coney Island boardwalk is often used as a signifier of mid-century America, when the area was fun and playful. Being at Coney meant a happy day by the ocean playing carny-style games, eating cotton candy and enjoying the summer breeze. It was one of the few places to offer relief in the summer in the days before air conditioning was a mainstay in most businesses and homes. Until the 1950s, it was seen as a safe and fun place to enjoy with your friends and family.

Neil Simon's 1986 play *Brighton Beach Memoirs* features Jonathan Silverman as Eugene Jerome, based on Simon's life growing up in the peninsula area near Coney Island. Eugene is a typical preteen kid obsessed with baseball, girls and becoming a writer in pre–World War II New York.

In *Enemies, A Love Story* (1989), directed by Brooklyn native Paul Mazursky, set in Coney Island in 1949, Holocaust survivor Herman Broder (Ron Silver) finds himself married to three women at once, with two of his wives simultaneously pregnant. Coney Island is "home" and is also a symbol of the future. With Lena Olin and Anjelica Huston.

Heaven Help Us (1985) stars Andrew McCarthy and Mary Stuart Masterson as JFK-era teenagers who fall in love under the boardwalk of Coney Island.

The landmark film *The Little Fugitive* (1953) was co-written and directed by Ray Ashley, Morris Engel and Ruth Orkin. It tells the story of a seven-year-old boy (eight-year-old non-actor Richie Andrusco) running away to Coney Island because he believes that he accidentally shot and killed his older brother (played by Richard Brewster). The naturalistic acting and direction capture mid-century New York City beautifully, and it is considered one of the precursors to the 1960s New Wave movement in film. Stanley Kubrick and Jean-Luc Godard were big fans of this movie. The directors each had a 35 mm camera strapped to their bodies, hidden to catch real visitors to the beach behaving unselfconsciously.

The Lords of Flatbush (1974)

Before Henry Winkler became leather jacket–wearing Arthur "Fonzie" Fonzarelli on TV's *Happy Days*, he played a Brooklyn street tough alongside a pre-*Rocky* Sylvester Stallone in *The Lords of Flatbush*. Their gang is based in the Flatbush section of Brooklyn, and while some of the scenes were filmed there, the Coney Island boardwalk also plays into the script, with Abraham Lincoln High School (located at 2800 Ocean Parkway) serving as the

Henry Winkler, Perry King, Sylvester Stallone and Paul Mace in *The Lords of Flatbush* (1974). *Columbia Pictures PictureLux, The Hollywood Archive/ Alamy Stock Photo.*

setting for the high school. It also features Susan Blakely and Maria Smith and music by Jamie Carr.

New York is an interesting beast on film. The adage "If you can make it here, you can make it anywhere" has been said about the city, but I always read that in another way—"Not many people can make it here."

My point is that to an observer who never experienced egg creams or stickball firsthand, New York is undoubtedly a beacon but an intimidating one. When I revisited The Lords of Flatbush, *the movie's title stood out to me. Instead of "The Lords" being an aggressive signifier for the rough-and-tumble gang representing Flatbush, I read it as a wistful "The Lords," a gang that existed in Flatbush, made a tiny dent, and now lives on in the memory of a small inner circle. It fits the movie because* The Lords of Flatbush *feels like a memory piece; scenes are shapeless and meandering, feeling more like half-memories of an experience than happening at the moment.*

*This is one of the film's strengths because though it feels slight in length (a brisk eighty-three minutes) and scale (this was an independent production picked up by a major studio, Columbia Pictures), it closes with a great deal of resonance that sneaks up on the viewer. The lasting impressions are the great performances from the likes of baby-faced pre-*Rocky *Sylvester Stallone, Henry Winkler, Perry King and Paul Mace and the firecracker ladies in their lives, including Susan Blakely and Maria Smith. Stallone and Smith share the best moment in the movie—an awkward engagement ring transaction at a local jeweler which should be studied in comedy workshops for its writing, pacing and histrionics. I also quite like the music* *in the film, especially "Chico's Song (You and Me)" and "Wedding Day," performed beautifully by Jamie Carr.*

After you finish the movie, read the IMDb trivia for the film. There's a hilarious story about the on-set rivalry between Stallone and Richard Gere, who was originally in the cast before being fired from the production.
—*Adam Riske, senior writer of FThisMovie.com*

CONEY ISLAND CYCLONE

The Coney Island Cyclone, 801 Riegelmann Boardwalk, July 2021.

The infamous Coney Island Cyclone is a wooden roller coaster rite of passage for many visitors to Luna Park. Erected in 1927, the Cyclone has a scary history for its sheer pace and rickety-ness. World-famous aviator Charles Lindbergh declared the ride even more exhilarating than being at top speed in the air in 1929. It's so fast, and how one doesn't fly out of it is one of its many old-fashioned charms. In 1991, it was listed in the National Register of Historic Places, and it was renewed and refurbished in 2016.

It is the location for 1978's *The Wiz* (an African American musical retelling of *The Wizard of Oz* by L. Frank Baum), where Diana Ross (as a thirty-two-year-old Dorothy) meets Michael Jackson playing the Scarecrow on their way to Oz at the Cyclone.

The Cyclone is also the setting for Woody Allen's *Annie Hall* (1977); his family lives right next to the famous Thunderbolt roller coaster. He recalls entire conversations and arguments with his family where the house would rattle when the ride was in action.

The Thunderbolt roller coaster was initially a wooden track ride from 1925 to 1982 and eventually fell into disrepair. It was rebuilt in 2014 and sits at Luna Park near Surf Avenue and West 15th Street.

The Cyclone in action, July 2021.

THE WONDER WHEEL

The Wonder Wheel Ferris wheel was built in 1920 just as the IRT subways finally reached Coney Island, bringing millions of visitors. This ride was unique, as the cars moved along a track as the wheel turned with perfect views of New York City. It has the distinction of being named a city landmark in 1989 and having an excellent safety record.

In 1985's *Remo Williams: The Adventure Begins*, trained assassin Remo Williams (played by Fred Ward) and Joel Grey, who plays his elderly Asian mentor/sensei (it was the '80s!), meet at the Wonder Wheel before taking off on an adventure to save the president of the United States.

In 2008's *Cloverfield*, Coney Island is where the leads, Michael Stahl-David and Odette Annable, film part of their date at the Wonder Wheel, inadvertently recording the moment a satellite crashes into the Atlantic Ocean. It's unknown how well the boardwalk holds up after the attack.

The iconic Ferris wheel is often used as a backdrop to show that a film's characters are indeed in Coney Island, such as in 2017's *Spider-Man: Homecoming*, when Tom Holland as Peter Parker faces off against Michael Keaton's Vulture.

Also in 2017 was the movie *Wonder Wheel*, starring Kate Winslet, Justin Timberlake and Juno Temple and directed by Woody Allen, whom Winslet

The entrance for the Deno's Wonder Wheel Amusement Park, 3059 West 12th Street, July 2021.

would later say she regretted working with due to the allegations of sexual abuse by his daughter in the early 1990s. The Wonder Wheel plays front and center to the plot and the imagery, as the lead characters live across the street from the attraction.

In the 1980s, Coney Island was in a state of disrepair. The rides were out of date, broken down or just plain abandoned, as witnessed in several films set on or near the boardwalk at the time. For sheer over-the-top stunts (including a scene where a car on the Cyclone flies off the rails), you need to see 1988's *Shakedown* with Peter Weller and Sam Elliott taking on dirty cops in New York City.

Angel Heart, directed by Alan Parker (*The Commitments* and *Mississippi Burning*) with Mickey Rourke and Robert DeNiro, caused a massive stir in 1987 when released due to graphic sex scenes between Rourke and Lisa Bonet. The first part of the film depicts 1950s Brooklyn and Coney Island. Mickey Rourke would later claim that DeNiro hated working with him so much that he was denied a role in 2019's *The Irishman*, starring DeNiro and directed by Martin Scorsese. (*The Irishman* producers deny this.)

Also in 1987, *The Pick-Up Artist* by controversial writer/director James Toback (accused by over thirty women of sexual harassment) stars Robert Downey Jr. (billed for the last time in his career as Robert Downey) and Molly Ringwald (the actor's first "adult" role at eighteen) as two addicts who fall in love. He can't help but chase women and collect their phone numbers, and she is in debt protecting her alcoholic father (played by Dennis Hopper) and owes $25,000 to bookie Harvey Keitel because of her gambling habit. The social politics are not great, but it offers incredible views of New York City in the mid-1980s, and Ringwald's dingy apartment on Coney Island looks authentic.

Brittany Murphy plays a fun Manhattan party girl in charge of Dakota Fanning—a somber eight-year-old—in 2003's *Uptown Girls*. Their

The Wonder Wheel view from the boardwalk, July 2021.

characters escape to the Coney Island boardwalk to try the teacup rides in one of the scenes.

Coney Island was given a more romantic treatment in Sandra Bullock's *Two Weeks Notice* (2002), co-starring Hugh Grant. Grant plays a gruff boss to sweet Bullock, who, because of his constant demands on her time, leaves her job with his promise that he will not destroy the "Coney Island Community Center," which is her pet cause. He reneges on this but soon has a change of heart (#lovewins). The site (now called the Ford Amphitheater at Coney Island) has been declared a New York Landmark and is located on West 21st Street at the Riegelmann Boardwalk at Coney Island.

Nathan's Hot Dogs

Started in 1916 by Polish immigrant Nathan Handwerker, Nathan's Hot Dogs at 1310 Surf Avenue is an institution that draws thousands of hungry visitors per day and holds an annual hot dog–eating contest, usually won by competitive eater Joey Chestnut, known as "Jaws." (He scarfed down seventy-six hot dogs in ten minutes in 2021.) You can find Nathan's in the background of several movies like Spike Lee's 1998 *He Got Game* and Adam

Nathan's Hot Dogs, 1310 Surf Avenue, July 2021.

McKay's 2010 film *The Other Guys* starring Will Farrell and Mark Wahlberg. Mark's brother, chef Paul Wahlberg, would open a Wahlburgers restaurant (a burger franchise with a signature "Wahl Sauce") directly across the street from there in 2018.

Coney Island (1917)

Alice Mann, Roscoe "Fatty" Arbuckle and Buster Keaton in *Coney Island* (1917).

Roscoe "Fatty" Arbuckle was one of the most famous comedic actors of the silent screen era—until a scandal in San Francisco in 1921. After an incident in a hotel room bathtub adjacent to his, a partygoer died, and Arbuckle was charged in the death. Arbuckle, who was tried three times and always acquitted, never recovered. This was one of the critical incidents to bring about the "Hays Code" in 1930, which was meant to clean up a supposedly immoral Hollywood. Nowadays, we would say he was "canceled."

In 1917, Fatty was directing his films to great success, including *Coney Island*, which you can find on YouTube. There is also a 1943 film with the same title starring Betty Grable that is set in but not filmed at Coney Island. It also features blackface dancers, so content warning about 1940s racism.

CONEY ISLAND MOVIES

- *A.I. Artificial Intelligence* (2001) This is a Steven Spielberg sci-fi story with Jude Law and Haley Joel Osment.
- *Angel Heart* (1987) This weird psychological story is about a private investigator (Mickey Rourke); the "devil," Robert DeNiro (spoiler); and Lisa Bonet with a controversial (at the time) sex scene.
- *Annie Hall* (1977) Woody Allen takes his friends back to Brooklyn to explain his childhood.
- *Beaches* (1988) C.C. and Hillary meet at the boardwalk when they are children. Adorable.
- *Boardwalk* (1979) A depressing story about an elderly couple (Ruth Gordon and Lee Strasberg) being scared out of their Coney Island home by gangs.
- *Brighton Beach Memoirs* (1986) The beginning of a Neil Simon trilogy that delights.
- *Brooklyn* (2015) A love story about an Irish girl who meets an Italian boy.
- *Bullet* (1996) Mickey Rourke, Adrien Brody and Tupac Shakur in a film about drugs and violence.
- *Bye Bye Braverman* (1968) Four men (including George Segal and Jack Warden) drive around New York to attend a funeral.
- *Cloverfield* (2008) The world being attacked by monsters begins at the Cyclone!
- *Coney Island* (1917) and (1943) The first is a Fatty Arbuckle short film with Buster Keaton, and the second is a Betty Grable musical.
- *The Crowd* (1928) King Vidor directs this film about existing in an "impersonal metropolis."
- *Demolition* (2015) Jake Gyllenhaal's drama about a man coping with his wife's death.
- *Enemies, A Love Story* (1989) Paul Mazursky's classic film about love and loss in post–World War II America.

- *Goodfellas* (1990) Gangsters kill and curse their way around New York.
- *Heaven Help Us* (1985) Kids in the 1960s/JFK-era America try to navigate life with strict Catholic schools and their raging hormones.
- *He Got Game* (1998) Denzel Washington plays a man trying to get his son (Ray Allen) to attend college on a basketball scholarship.
- *Hell Up in Harlem* (1973) Fred Williamson is a gangster trying to rescue his ex from the mafia.
- *The Little Fugitive* (1953) A little boy (played by seven-year-old Richie Andrusco) runs away from home after believing he killed his older brother. It is considered one of the most influential films of the 1950s and utilizes an early version of the Steadicam.
- *Little Odessa* (1995) Tim Roth lives with his Soviet Jewish family in Brighton Beach
- *Lord of War* (2005) Nicolas Cage is an arms dealer with Ethan Hawke and Jared Leto.
- *Men in Black 3* (2012) The agents are in 1969 trying to fix an assassination.
- *The Object of My Affection* (1998) A problematic film about a heterosexual woman (Jennifer Aniston) who falls in love with her best friend, who is homosexual (Paul Rudd).
- *The Other Guys* (2010) Will Farrell and Mark Wahlberg's comedy is partly filmed here and is exceptionally OK.
- *Out for Justice* (1991) Steven Seagal flips people and solves crime.
- *Over the Brooklyn Bridge* (1984) An Elliott Gould romance that is very 1980s in look and attitude.
- *Percy Jackson and the Olympians: The Lightning Thief* (2010) A teen realizes he is a Greek god.
- *Pi* (1997) Darren Aronofsky's first film was an art-house darling and filmed on the sly here.
- *The Pickle* (1993) Danny Aiello is a Hollywood director who needs to produce a hit.
- *The Pick-Up Artist* (1987) Robert Downey Jr. aggressively chases women and strikes gold with Molly Ringwald.
- *Radio Days* (1987) A lovely film by Woody Allen about his love of swing music and radio as a child. Stars Mia Farrow, Dianne

Luna Park in Coney Island, 1000 Surf Avenue, July 2021.

Wiest, Julie Kavner, Seth Green, Michael Tucker and Josh Mostel.

- *Remo Williams: The Adventure Begins* (1985) This action hit stars Fred Ward, who learns to be an assassin by expert "Korean" trainer Chiun (Joel Grey; it was the '80s!).
- *Requiem for a Dream* (2000) This movie is brilliant and a stone-cold bummer about addiction with Jennifer Connelly and Marlon Wayans.
- *Romeo Is Bleeding* (1994) A stylish action film with Gary Oldman and Lena Olin.
- *Shakedown* (1988) A totally bananas '80s-era "buddy cop" film with Peter Weller and Sam Elliott that has a shootout on the Cyclone!
- *Sophie's Choice* (1983) A beautiful film and a very tough exploration of love, loss, and abuse.
- *Speedy* (1928) Harold Lloyd and Babe Ruth were massive stars in their day and star in this tale about baseball and horse-drawn trolleys.

Bump Your Ass Off! Eldorado bumper cars, 1216 Surf Avenue.

- *Spider-Man: Homecoming* (2017) Tom Holland is our webbed hero, and Michael Keaton plays Vulture. They fight on the sand by the Wonder Wheel.
- *Two Weeks Notice* (2002) When Sandra Bullock quits, her boss, Hugh Grant, realizes he loves her.
- *Uptown Girls* (2003) Brittany Murphy and Dakota Fanning spend a day at Coney Island.
- *The Warriors* (1979) I am team Baseball Furies.
- *Went to Coney Island on a Mission from God…Be Back by Five* (1998) Jon Cryer wrote and starred in this indie production directed by Richard Schenkman.
- *We Own the Night* (2007) Joaquin Phoenix and Mark Wahlberg star in this thriller.
- *When Harry Met Sally* (1987) Billy Crystal (Harry) and Bruno Kirby (Baby Fish Mouth) hang out at a batting cage near the boardwalk.
- *The Wiz* (1978) Diana Ross plays Dorothy, who meets Michael Jackson (the Scarecrow) at the Cyclone in this update of *The Wizard of Oz*.

Rick Stear and Jon Cryer in *Went to Coney Island on a Mission from God…Back by Five*, 1998. *Photo by Tom Legoff.*

- *Wolfen* (1981) Edward James Olmos (Holt) takes his clothes off while at the beach and stalks around the pier as he is possessed by a wolf-like entity.
- *Wonder* (2017) A boy (played by Jacob Tremblay) with facial differences hangs out on the pier, and Julia Roberts and Owen Wilson play his parents.
- *Wonder Wheel* (2017) Stars Kate Winslet, Juno Temple, Tony Sirico and Justin Timberlake.

CHAPTER 5

GRITTY BROOKLYN

"How You Doin'?"

Would ya watch the hair? You know, I work on my hair a long time, and you hit it. He hits my hair.
—*Tony Manero (John Travolta) in* Saturday Night Fever

The very sound of the word *Brooklyn* is tough and gritty to the ears. It's derived from Dutch settlers who used it from their hometown Breukelen, the Netherlands (which means "Broken Land"). It's home to every type of ethnicity with a reputation for being one of the places immigrants start in America before they move on. Betty Smith wrote about her childhood in the early part of the twentieth century in Williamsburg in *A Tree Grows in Brooklyn*, which describes a hard life of tenement living and fighting for work among your peers.

Movies helped spread Brooklyn's reputation as just a little rougher and more resilient than most cities, and this chapter is about some of the most popular stories, characters and places in film history.

Karen Lynn Gorney and John Travolta in *Saturday Night Fever* (1977). *A.F. Archive/Alamy Stock Photo.*

Coming to America (1988)

This Eddie Murphy movie is one of the most successful comedies of the 1980s and was directed by John Landis. It is about a pampered African prince who is looking for his true love. It's hard to avoid the charms of Prince Akeem (Murphy) and Semmi (Arsenio Hall), who come to America to find a wife in Queens.

This movie was a massive hit for Murphy, and while most of the film takes place in other boroughs, for Akeem's apartment and the barbershop scenes, John Landis used a pre-hipster building in Williamsburg at 392 South 5th Street.

392 South 5th Street (Williamsburg), "Hipster Heaven" these days, but it was quite rough in the '80s. July 2021.

The Departed (2006)

Martin Scorsese directed Jack Nicholson and Leonardo DiCaprio in this ultra-violent tale of a Boston mob boss taking over the police force from the inside. Much of the film took place in Boston. Still, in Brooklyn, Fernando's Focacceria at 151 Union Street in Cobble Hill, the "Irish Haven" at 5724 4th Avenue in Sunset Park and the "lobster scene" at Tamaqua Bar and Marina at 84 Ebony Court in Gerritsen Beach stood in for the "Beantown" area.

Left: *The Departed* (2006), a Warner Brothers film with Leonardo DiCaprio (*left*) and Jack Nicholson. *Pictorial Press LTD/Alamy Stock Photo.*

Right, top and bottom: Fernando's Focacceria (from *The Departed*), 151 Union Street (Cobble Hill), March 2022.

Dog Day Afternoon (1975)

Top: Al Pacino and Penelope Allen in *Dog Day Afternoon*. (1975). *Wikimedia*.

Bottom: Site of *Dog Day Afternoon* today, 279 Prospect Park West (Windsor Terrace).

Based on a true story, Sidney Lumet's film takes place almost entirely in one location, a Brooklyn bank that is the scene of a robbery gone awry. Al Pacino plays Sonny (based on real-life John Wojtowicz), an amateur crook looking to fund a sex-reassignment surgery for his partner Leon (in real life known as Elizabeth Eden) when he takes a bank full of employees hostage. The media circus that ensues resembles real-life events on August 22, 1972, at a Chase Bank in the Gravesend section of Brooklyn. It stars an amazing cast, including John Cazale, Carol Kane, James Broderick (father of Matthew) and Charles Durning. In one of the crowd scenes, you can see a young Harvey Fierstein as an extra.

The outdoor scenes for the movie were filmed in Windsor Terrace at 279 Prospect Park West, which is now home to private residences. In the film, a crowd gathers to take in the spectacle, with one memorable scene having Al Pacino yell "Attica!" as a reference to the famous prison riot of September 9, 1971. This is also what Tony Manero says to his grandmother when she catches him in his underwear in *Saturday Night Fever*.

Photographer Victor Kemper recalled in *Making Movies* by Sidney Lumet:

> *The first decision was that we use no artificial light. Fluorescents lighted the bank in the ceiling. Outside, all the light came from the enormous spotlights of the Police Emergency van on the scene at night. And for the improvised scenes in the street and the bank, I used two and sometimes three hand-held cameras to reinforce the documentary feel.*

Clever business owners Joe Boyle and Jay Kerr created a Chicago-style hot dog place filled with movie paraphernalia and a boss Ms. Pac-Man game called Dog Day Afternoon across from the film's original location. It has a polish sausage worth walking a mile in the rain for—a mustardy delight!

Donnie Brasco (1997)

Johnny Depp stars as an FBI informant who infiltrates the mafia of early 1970s New York City and befriends Al Pacino's Lefty, who is on the fringes of power of the families at the time. It also stars Bruno Kirby, Michael Madsen and Anne Heche. For one scene, a rundown Park Slope diner on the corner of 9th Street at 8th Avenue was used, and minimal art direction was needed to achieve a

Site of a scene from *Donnie Brasco*, 511 9th Street (Park Slope).

dirty look. Soon after the film came out, the location turned into a chic diner that for twenty years had lines for brunch every weekend until the pandemic in 2020. Today, it serves as a family-friendly bodega.

The French Connection (1971)

This semi-true story of New York City narcotics officers who busted a drug-smuggling ring run by a syndicate based in France, Canada and the United States became the surprise hit of 1971, winning several Academy Awards, including Best Picture, Best Director (William Friedkin) and Best Actor (Gene Hackman). It features some of the most exciting action sequences on film, including one infamous car chase considered one of the best in movie history.

Hackman plays Jimmy "Popeye" Doyle, a narcotics officer based in Brooklyn who is obsessed with the French bringing heroin to New York in the late 1960s. Roy Scheider plays his partner, Russo. He starts chasing an assassin through Brooklyn on an elevated train heading to Manhattan. Popeye takes over a car from a civilian (he establishes himself entirely above the law several times in the film) and, on the road, follows the train from Stillwell Avenue/86th Street to just north of the 62nd Street station.

The sequence involves several minor collisions and (supposedly) close calls directed by the ambitious Friedkin, who claimed for years that he had no permits and let his stunt drivers run loose throughout the Bay Ridge neighborhood. However, according to his biography, *The Friedkin Connection: A Memoir*, the chase scenes culminated in several highly choreographed runs

63rd Street from *The French Connection*'s infamous chase scene, Stilwell Avenue (Bay Ridge).

weighed down with cameras and off-duty police warning inadvertent extras to avoid getting hit by the 1971 Pontiac LeMans. He wrote, "To achieve the effect of Popeye's car narrowly missing the woman with a baby carriage, I had a camera mounted with three cameras on different lenses drive slowly toward a stuntwoman. We changed the camera speed to fast motion."

A pivotal scene in *The French Connection* shows Popeye shooting an assassin as he attempts to flee from the 62nd Street station. Supposedly, this did not happen in real life, but Friedkin thought it was true to the character of Eddie Egan, the real-life person on whom the character of Popeye is based and who agreed with the brash director. The scene would become famous as the poster for the film. Today, you can walk around the neighborhood, which has changed very little since the film's release.

The Godfather (1972)

Francis Ford Coppola's treatment of the Mario Puzo novel was a massive hit in 1972 and is one of the most-watched films in cable TV history. (Seriously, it seems to be playing along with the sequel *The Godfather 2* on a loop in the cable-verse!) With fantastic performances by Marlon Brando, Al Pacino, John Cazale, Robert Duvall and James Caan (to name a few) and some of the most quotable lines ever invented ("I'm going to make him an offer he can't refuse"), *The Godfather* is a masterclass of filmmaking. You can find a few locations in Brooklyn used for crucial scenes in the film.

Luca Brasi (played by former wrestler Lenny Montana) meets his fate as an enforcer for the Corleone family at Hotel St. George in Brooklyn Heights at 100 Henry Street.

And as hitman Peter Clemenza (Richard S. Castellano) leaves his home in Gravesend before taking out stool pigeon Paulie Gatto (John Martino), he

Left: Site where Luca Brasi in *The Godfather* began sleeping with the fishes, 100 Henry Street (Brooklyn Heights), May 2021.

Right: Location for Clemenza's home: "Don't forget the cannoli!" 1999 East 5th Street (Gravesend), July 2021.

is reminded by his wife, "Don't forget the cannoli!" You can see his home at 1999 East 5th Street, which maintains its mid-twentieth-century charm in a quiet neighborhood.

> The Godfather *is the I Ching. It is the sum of all wisdom.* The Godfather *is the answer to any question. What should I pack for my summer vacation? Leave the gun, take the cannoli. What day of the week is it? Monday, Tuesday, Thursday, Wednesday…*
> —*Tom Hanks as Joe Fox in 1998's* You've Got Mail,
> *written by Norah Ephron and Delia Ephron*

Goodfellas (1990)

One of Martin Scorsese's most beloved films is the story of real-life gangster Henry Hill (played brilliantly by Ray Liotta), whose memoirs inspired the screenplay and direction of the movie. Born and raised in the Brownsville section of Brooklyn, Henry started his life of crime with the Lucchese mob in 1955 (when he was twelve) and continued until 1980, when he became a rat and informed to the FBI on his cohorts in narcotics for murdering people. Before going into the Witness Protection Program, Henry's testimonies in court helped put away several mobsters, including James Burke (called James "Jimmy" Conway and played by Robert DeNiro in the film).

Top: Tommy's (Joe Pesci's) in *Goodfellas* "made man" location at 5 East 80th Street (Bay Ridge), March 2022.

Middle: *Goodfellas* location, 5 East 80th Street (Bay Ridge) March 2022.

Below: Scene with "Jimmy and Karen" in *Goodfellas*, Smith and 9th Streets (Carroll Gardens), March 2022.

Brooklyn was a location for several key scenes that you can visit, including the Oriental Manor, which was the location of Henry and Karen Hill's (Lorraine Bracco) wedding at 1818 86th Street in the Bath Beach section of Brooklyn. The home where Joe Pesci's character Tommy DeVito thinks he will be a "made man" is in Bay Ridge at 5 80th Street, by Shore Road.

The scene where Jimmy "offers" Karen free dresses and she flees in a panic is right by the Smith and 9th Street subway stop that at the time was abandoned and most definitely not a safe place for a woman to be alone. These days, it has new shops and a family-friendly park with a dog run and track.

Smith Street in Red Hook is the setting for several Jimmy Conway meetings, including those with the younger Henry Hill and his soon-to-be best friend Tommy DeVito, which earned Pesci an Academy Award for Best Supporting Actor in 1991.

The Hot Rock (1972)

One of Australian filmmaker Peter Yates's (*Bullit, Breaking Away*) first movies in Brooklyn, *The Hot Rock* is a caper starring Robert Redford, George Segal and Moses Gunn about thieves looking to steal an African diamond from an exhibit at the Brooklyn Museum.

The Brooklyn Museum, 200 Eastern Parkway (Prospect Heights), July 2022.

Based on a novel by David E. Westlake, with screenplay by William F. Goldman *(Butch Cassidy and the Sundance Kid, The Princess Bride)*, music by Quincy Jones and a loopy performance by Zero Mostel, *The Hot Rock* is a cult classic for fans of '70s ensemble/heist movies. Watching *The Hot Rock* with a modern lens, it's astonishing how much access was granted at the time for the filming. A car is crashed right in front of the museum office door as a ruse!

The museum is located at 200 Eastern Parkway, and the entrance (which is now filled with giant steps) is close to Prospect Park, where the ragtag team gets together to plan the unusual burglary.

The Hot Rock is a heist movie. I love heist movies. As a kid, I wanted to be a cat burglar. They are trying to steal a diamond from the Brooklyn

63

Museum. It's not the Brooklyn of today. It's the Brooklyn of 1972, where I assume you could have just walked into the Brooklyn Museum and taken what you wanted.

I think that part of me that loves to see old New York, whether you are watching a movie like that or The Taking of Pelham 1, 2, 3, *you see these images of '70s New York that are very fun.*

—*Wyatt Cenac (comedian and actor),*
Adventures in Movie Going *(Criterion Channel)*

Notorious (2009)

Mural of Notorious
B.I.G. at 694 Fulton
Street (Fort Greene),
June 2021. *Creative
Commons Attribution/
Elhesinberg.*

Christopher "Biggie" Wallace was a hip-hop superstar who performed under the name the Notorious B.I.G. and is considered one of the best rappers. He was born and raised in Brooklyn at 226 St. James Place in Clinton Hill, and his murder at the age of twenty-four (still unsolved at the time of this printing) has only increased his fame. The movie, directed by George Tillman Jr., was based on his life (with Jamal Woolard as Wallace) in Brooklyn, including Fulton Street and St. James Street—Biggie's old stomping grounds.

Once Upon a Time in America (1984)

Italian director Sergio Leoni (famous for his spaghetti Westerns) took on the gangster genre by adapting author Harry Grey's *The Hoods*, based on his own life experiences witnessing early twentieth-century New York City syndicates. At over three and a half hours in length, it tells a long and languid story about gangsters David "Noodles" Aaronson (Robert DeNiro) and Maximillian "Max" Bercovicz (James Woods), who are partners and rivals, and the various loves and crimes in their lives. It is the film debut of Jennifer Connelly and features performances by Joe Pesci, Elizabeth McGovern and Danny Aiello. At the beginning of the film, a sequence involving a group of recent immigrants crossing Water Street is considered a modern classic. Much of the film used areas of then degenerate Williamsburg for the character of Noodles, including his home

Manhattan Bridge Tower in Brooklyn by Danny Lyon, June 1974. *Public domain via the Environmental Protection Agency.*

at 105 South 8th Street and Moe's Bar at 95 South 8th Street.

According to Tony Sokol in 2021 for *Den of Geek*, this film (in his opinion) is as great as *The Godfather* in terms of attention to detail, such as "DeNiro's stirring a cup of coffee or the character of Patsy (played by James Hayden) enjoying a pastry over sex. Leoni's characters have joyful and pleasurable moments, mostly missing in other gangster films. *Once Upon a Time in America* ripped the genre's insides out and displayed them with unflinching veracity and theatrical beauty. It is a perfect film, gorgeously shot, masterfully timed, and slightly ajar."

Saturday Night Fever (1977)

In the mid-1970s, British writer Nic Cohn struggled with his identity as a gay man and often prowled the nightclubs in the outer boroughs (Brooklyn, Queens, Staten Island and the Bronx) that seemed freer in spirit and more expressive than Manhattan. Openly gay men could dance to disco music with their fellow citizens of every nationality without fear of reprisal, for the most part. (Brooklyn is/was very Catholic and religious, but Brooklynites support the LGBTQ community.)

Cohn's June 1976 *New York* magazine article "Tribal Rights of the New Saturday Night" told the story of a nineteen-year-old Italian American named Vincent, who worked at a paint shop and dreamed of leaving his Bay Ridge neighborhood to live over the bridge in Manhattan and leave his small world behind. For decades, Manhattanites included Brooklyn in the very not-so-equal world of "bridge and tunnel" people, a slur that doesn't exist so much now that Brooklyn is one of the most expensive (and inclusive) places in New York.

A rising star named John Travolta, seen by millions of people every week on TV's *Welcome Back, Kotter*, was given a party to celebrate his taking the lead in the newly titled *Saturday Night Fever*. The now-named Tony Manero would play a tough Bay Ridge young man who hangs out at a local disco called 2001 Odyssey with brutal friends who have strict rules on living and behaving.

Costars include Barry Miller (Bobby C.), Joseph Cali (Joey), Paul Pape (Double J.), Donna Pescow (Annette), Karen Lynn Gorney (Stephanie) and Martin Shakar, who plays Tony's brother Frank Jr., who is leaving the priesthood.

Visiting *Saturday Night Fever* with a modern eye can be a jolt to the system. The racism, sexism, homophobia and bleak outlook on life in the 1970s are peppered throughout the story. Director John Badham wanted to show the several different worlds that existed in a seemingly small community in Bay Ridge and how they either united or clashed over music, religion and being poor and working class in a city that seemed it would soon end up in ruins.

There is an undeniable joy here as well, with the soundtrack full of some of the best dance music from the era. You can still find many of the places used as locations in the movie, including the opening scene of Tony walking on 86th Street in Bensonhurst. (John Travolta's body double was the person's boot you see rising in the opening credits.)

Lenny's Pizza Parlor still exists at 1969 86th Street, and you can still attempt to eat it the Tony Manero way (a tight disco pants–busting two slices at once!). The dance studio is closed, but the building is at 1301 West 7th Street. In Bay Ridge, the Manero family home is still standing at 221 79th Street, and you can play basketball at John J. Carty Park nearby.

Tony's paint shop is still in business under Pearson Paint & Hardware at

Top: The site of the 2001 Odyssey Disco, 802 64th Street (Bay Ridge), June 2021.

Middle: Lenny's Pizza from *Saturday Night Fever*, 1969 86th Street (Bensonhurst), June 2021.

Bottom: The *Saturday Night Fever* home at 221 79th Street (Bay Ridge), June 2021.

7305 5th Avenue in Bay Ridge. The 2001 Odyssey Disco, located at 802 64th Street in the 1970s and 1980s (and surrounded by gangs that threatened the crew with firebombs during the film shoot), is gone after going through several owners. It is now a multiuse building in a thriving part of the Chinese American community.

There are no pedestrian walkways on the Verrazano-Narrows Bridge, and I don't suggest getting out of your car to play, as they do in the film. But there are several places in the Bay Ridge neighborhood to stroll around and enjoy the local flavor.

I was a kid when Fever *exploded like a rocket into the stratosphere. I was already familiar with John Travolta from his hit TV show* Welcome Back Kotter. *But nothing, like nothing, prepared me for what* Saturday Night Fever *not only did to America and the world but to me emotionally, spiritually and physically. I was captivated; I wanted to dance, too; I wanted to be admired like he was for something I was great at too. I was so young that I did not understand the intersections of race, gender and gender violence, class and even homophobia in various parts of the film.*

That would come years later, and in many ways, Fever *would foreshadow the insulated white working-class Americans who would wind up being anti-immigrant, anti–gay rights, anti–voting rights and anti-abortion Trump supporters. The seeds are there in this film, and only Travolta's character can see them, which is why he wants to free himself from it all. Yes, this resonated with me because Tony Manero, as played by Travolta, was on a quest for freedom through dance and music. The effect of* Fever *was so potent that to this very day, if I see John Travolta's name in any way, I stop, just to see and hear. Few characters and films in my lifetime have had a greater effect on me.*

—Kevin Powell, poet, journalist, civil and human rights activist and biographer of Tupac Shakur

There is a plethora of Brooklyn locations used to demonstrate the grit of the various neighborhoods throughout the borough.

- *Above the Rim* (1994) A high school basketball star and his family make up this drama, filmed at Samuel J. Tilden High School (East Flatbush).
- *Bullet* (1996) One of Tupac Shakur's last movie roles before his murder. The Cypress Hills Cemetery was used for a scene.

- *Dead Presidents* (1995) A Vietnam vet gets involved in crime that partly takes place Noble Street and West Street (Greenpoint). Stars Larenz Tate, Keith David and Chris Tucker.
- *Glengarry Glen Ross* (1992) The main office for the salesmen of Premiere Properties was at 1515 Sheepshead Bay Road, and China Bowl restaurant was at 1520 Sheepshead Bay Road in Sheepshead Bay. With Alec Baldwin, Al Pacino and Jack Lemmon.
- *Romeo Is Bleeding* (1993) Filmed at Myrtle Avenue and Bleecker Avenue (Bushwick). Gary Oldman plays a dirty New York City cop, and Lena Olin is an improbably pretty Russian assassin.
- *Sleepers* (1996) Crime drama with Brad Pitt and Robert DeNiro that is a tough watch about child abuse and revenge. The Most Holy Trinity Church (138 Montrose Avenue in Williamsburg) and Greenpoint was used for a scene.
- *The Super* (1991) A shot that takes place at a Brooklyn bodega is at 1158 Myrtle Avenue (Bushwick). Joe Pesci plays a landlord for a property on a building that is for sure expensive now but was a hovel then. Hilarity does *not* ensue.

CHAPTER 6

ROMANTIC BROOKLYN

"When the Moon Hits Your Eye..."

When the moon hits your eye like a big pizza pie, that's amore!
—Dean Martin

Is the feeling of falling in love the same as being in love? How can you tell when you're in love? Why do fools fall in love? These are some of the biggest questions in the world, and movies try to answer them with visuals, snappy (or sappy) dialogue and actors who bring words and emotions to life. The answers are just as funny, sad, beautiful and heartbreaking on celluloid as they are in life. Here are some locations for films that land directly in the hearts of movie audiences with romance on their minds.

The Age of Innocence (1993)

Prospect Park, Brooklyn (view from the Boathouse and Audubon), March 2022.

In this tragic Edith Wharton story, directed by Martin Scorsese, Newland Archer (Daniel Day-Lewis) falls in love with his cousin Ellen Olenska (Michelle Pfeiffer). For various reasons, due to the classicism and sexism of the early twentieth century, he must instead marry May Weiland (Winona Ryder). At one point, he bumps into Ellen, which provides romantic tension. Prospect Park served as a park in Boston, and Day-Lewis was spotted in character and on horseback in Park Slope on 8th Avenue between Carroll and President Streets.

Annie Hall (1977)

This is Woody Allen's 1977 love letter to the titular character, played by an incandescent Diane Keaton. There are several locations throughout Brooklyn used as markers for the growing relationship between Allen's Alvy Singer and Hall. The Brooklyn Bridge is featured as the meeting place to discuss life and love between the characters, who admit their growing attraction. At the same time, Coney Island, as Singer's home neighborhood, illustrates his chaotic upbringing with his family living up right next to the Cyclone roller coaster. The movie is filled with memorable scenes with up-and-coming stars like Jeff Goldblum, Carol Kane and Christopher Walken.

> *After graduating from college, I moved from Minnesota to New York. People often asked me: "Why New York?" and my answer was simple: Woody Allen. These days, of course, Woody Allen is seen as incredibly divisive (to say the least). Still, as a kid, I and much of the world saw him as a great arbiter of taste, a comic genius and a brilliant observer of cultural and class distinctions. Movies like* Annie Hall *showed a place in the world for weirdos who have no interest in the cheerleading squad or hockey team. I've now lived in New York for over twenty years (in Brooklyn the entire time), and to my delight, Woody Allen didn't lie. I belong here.*
> —*Kristen Meinzer,* Movie Therapy with Rafer and Kristen, *guest host for* NPR's Pop Culture Happy Hour *and culture critic*

Brooklyn (2015)

Saoirse Ronan plays Irish immigrant Eilis Lacey, who lands in 1950s Brooklyn to make a new life. While enjoying a romance with an Italian American, Tony Fiorello (Emory Cohen), she learns the joy of spending a day at Coney Island and how to eat spaghetti (with a spoon). Despite the name, most of the film was shot in more budget-friendly Quebec, with only two days devoted to actual shooting in New York. The brownstones on South Portland Avenue in Fort Greene served as the background for the exteriors of Eilis's boardinghouse and Coney Island for the day at the beach. John Crowley directed.

Shooting location for *Brooklyn* (2015), South Portland Avenue in Fort Greene, July 2021.

125 Prospect Park West (Park Slope), location for Barbra Streisand's character in *For Pete's Sake*.

For Pete's Sake (1974)

Barbra Streisand filmed many comedies in the 1970s. Still, none was as "zany" (as the movie poster stated) as this Peter Yates–directed movie that features Barbra playing a young, married woman (Henry) trying to protect her husband (Pete, played by Michael Sarazin) from financial ruin. We see Barbra don multiple wigs, ride a scooter through Park Slope and at one point round up a group of steers in Brooklyn Heights. Really! Their apartment was filmed at 125 Prospect Park West, which looks the same as in 1974.

Ghost (1990)

Oda Mae Brown (Whoopi Goldberg in 1990's *Ghost*) "psychic" parlor (the Verizon store was the location for the bodega in the film), 720 Franklin Avenue (Prospect Heights), September 2021.

In July 1990, *Ghost* was released to the world, and it became the number-one hit of the year with its combination of romance, comedy and action. It was directed by Jerry Zucker (*Top Secret* and *Ruthless People*). Patrick Swayze (Sam Wheat) and Demi Moore (Molly Jensen) play a couple who own a loft in SoHo and deeply love each other (though he can't seem to say "I love you") and have a bright future when Sam is killed during a robbery. Molly is grief-stricken as Sam becomes a spirit who lingers around her until she realizes he was set up for murder by his friend Carl Butler (Tony Goldwin). Sam hires spiritualist Oda Mae Brown (a hilarious Whoopi Goldberg in an Academy Award–winning performance). The latter can only hear him track down his killer and save Molly from harm before passing to the other side. As ridiculous as it all sounds, the movie works because the actors are doing their best work, and the scenes of New York City are vibrant and exciting.

Willie Lopez's (Rick Aviles in *Ghost*) apartment building, 592 Prospect Place (Prospect Heights), September 2021.

The film's special effects don't hold up so well, but the scenes of Moore crying became her big calling card. In her 2019 autobiography *Inside Out*, she writes about working with an acting coach because she didn't know if she could cry on cue in her real life. "That was the gem that film gave me—it pushed me to figure out how to access my emotions, particularly my pain. It had a huge impact on me and how I looked at myself."

The neighborhoods of Prospect Heights and Crown Heights (which have changed incredibly over the years into a haven of coffee shops and dog walkers aplenty) are the setting for Oda Mae's psychic parlor and apartment at 720 Franklin Avenue, as well as the home of Sam's killer, Willie Lopez (Rick Aviles), at 592 Prospect Place.

Ghost has a little bit of everything for everyone. You can watch it with anyone, and they'll find something they like. Do you like romance? Check. Do you like thrillers? Check. Do you want a supernatural element? Check. Do you like comedy? Here's Whoopi Goldberg at her Whoopi Goldbergiest.

Ghost feels like New York to me. Only in New York could a handsome finance guy and a beautiful artist afford to live in a massive, fantastic apartment. This particular loft in 1990 is considered a "fixer-upper." And only in New York could Oda Mae walk around talking to a ghost, and no one bats an eye.

—*Sonia Mansfield, co-host,* Dorking Out *and* What a Creep *podcasts*

Julie & Julia (2009)

This story about a food blogger who challenges herself to cook all of Julia Child's recipes is the last effort by writer and director Nora Ephron, who passed away in 2012. *Julie & Julia* features Meryl Streep as the famous chef and Stanley Tucci as her beloved husband, Paul Child, as they find a love for food and cooking while in Paris.

The location at 235 5th Avenue (Park Slope) stood in for in for a Paris café in *Julie & Julia*, September 2021.

Amy Adams plays writer Julia Powell in Queens, who, along with her loyal and patient husband, seeks to find herself out of the malaise of her life through the joy of cooking. The scenes of Streep and Tucci taking on the kitchens and restaurants in France (and taking holiday photos in their bathtub!) are incredibly joyful and romantic. The former Moutarde located at 5th Avenue and Union Street in Park Slope, was the stand-in for one of the film's locations meant to take place in Paris. Unfortunately, that restaurant is no longer (as of this publication) serving French cuisine. C'est la vie!

Moonstruck (1987)

Director Norman Jewison (*In the Heat of the Night*, *Fiddler on the Roof*) was looking for a romantic comedy when he came across the work of a playwright looking to break into movies—John Patrick Shanley. The original script, *The Bride and the Wolf*, told the story of a woman who has given up on finding true love and is willing to settle for someone who loves her but doesn't make her heart skip a beat. Enter his younger brother, who is missing a hand but sweeps her off her feet. Her complex Italian American family has their thoughts on love mixed in. Soon *Moonstruck* became the title, and it was one of the biggest hits of 1987.

Cher was offered the role of Loretta Castorini, but she initially refused due to her fear of mastering a Brooklyn accent. In his 2004 autobiography *This Terrible Business Has Been Good to Me*, Jewison recounts, "I told her, you're my first choice of any actress in this world. If you don't do this, you're going to regret it for the rest of your life."

The corner on Cranberry Street where Cher's character in *Moonstruck* dances home at dawn (Brooklyn Heights) August 2021.

Writer John Patrick Shanley, Norman Jewison and Olympia Dukakis, Canada Film Centre, 2011. *Creative Commons Attribution, Toronto International Film Festival.*

Nicolas Cage (who was considered a risky choice due to his previous box office showing) worked hard on his accent with the help of Danny Aiello, who would play his brother and Loretta's fiancé Johnny Cammareri. Aiello was happy for the break but later said he hated playing a "wimpy" role. Cher and Olympia Dukakis both won Academy Awards for their acting, and Shanley was recognized for best screenplay. (He would later win a Pulitzer Prize for the play *Doubt* in 2005.)

The sight of Cher dreamily walking home down Cranberry Street in Brooklyn Heights in 1987's *Moonstruck* is so iconic that movie fans worldwide visit the home of her character and her boisterous family. According to *Architectural Digest*, actor/comedian Amy Schumer reportedly paid $12.25 million in 2022 for the 1829 townhouse used for the exteriors of the film. Much of Clinton Hill, Carroll Gardens and Brooklyn Heights was used in the movie, including the Cammareri Bakery located at 502 Henry Street, which closed in 1998.

Jewison wrote in his book:

> *Because we couldn't count on Cosmo's* [Cher's father, played by Vincent Gardenia] *moon appearing on cue, David Watkin, our British director of photography, made us a portable moon of two hundred fay lights attached to a giant cherry picker. It could roll over the Manhattan skyline when we need it and cast its magical spell over the unlikely loves and betrayals of* Moonstruck.

Most of the film's interiors were shot in a film studio in Queens, but much around the Brooklyn neighborhoods remains the same, with the Brooklyn Promenade a five-minute walk away from the site of the Castorini home.

Left: The *Moonstruck* house, 19 Cranberry Street (Brooklyn Heights), 2021.

Below, left: The "Cammareri Bakery" at 502 Henry Street at Sackett in Cobble Hill, February 2022. *Photo by Nixon Thelusmond.*

Below, right: Vincent Gardenia and Cher in *Moonstruck* (1987). *APL Archive/Alamy Stock Photo.*

"Snap out of it!" I saw Moonstruck *before I'd ever been to New York, let alone Brooklyn. I remember seeing it with my parents in the movie theater at our local mall when it came out. I had seen many films set in Brooklyn by then, of course, but* Moonstruck *was the first film that made me ache to live there. For a start, there was that house! That enormous nineteenth-century house has beautiful woodwork, antiques and floor-to-ceiling subway tile in the kitchen. Nothing in my hometown of San Diego was that old, at least not with the original family still living there. In many ways, that house*

Vincent Gardenia Boulevard, 16th Avenue at 86th Street (Bensonhurst), June 2021. Gardenia (1920–1996) was an actor and Brooklyn resident for over sixty-eight years.

is one of the main characters. Right away, the audience is aware of all the history it must have seen, the tragedies and triumphs that had come and gone within its walls. Moonstruck *might be the most romantic movie ever because its romance survives despite death, infidelity, greed, pride, jealousy and time.*

There are so many iconic scenes in this movie, and it's still so funny. When I finally did move to New York (sadly, I never lived in Brooklyn, though I did get to attend grad school there), the lofty expectations Moonstruck *had set for me were completely fulfilled. Lincoln Center really is that magical in person. A morning stroll through old Brooklyn feels like the day is filled with possibilities—not just for you but for generations after you. Though I love every location, my favorite scene is still where Loretta tells her father that she will marry Johnny, the wrong man. The two of them sitting at the table in that tiled kitchen, toasting Loretta's terrible choice with a glass of Asti spumante, is as accurate a father-daughter relationship as I've ever seen on film. And it always makes me want to enjoy a glass of Asti with a sugar cube dropped in.*

—*Margo Porras, co-host,* Book Vs. Movie *podcast*

Sex and the City: The Movie (2008)

Miranda Hobbes and Steve Brady's relationship is an essential part of the suspense of the first *Sex and the City* film. Released in 2008, it features a penthouse with an enormous shoe closet, Carrie (Sarah Jessica Parker) hiring a personal assistant and Miranda creating havoc on Carrie's wedding day by telling Mr. Big (Chris Noth) that "marriage ruins everything." (Is this prescient for her character in the update …*And Just Like That*?!)

In the first film adaption of the series, though their relationship started on rocky ground, Miranda and Steve seem incredibly happy. The first film features a depressed Steve who cheats on Miranda and accuses her of being cold and distant. They decide to make up (see the Brooklyn Bridge section for those details) and raise their son Brady in Brooklyn.

In the original series, moving to Brooklyn was made to look like a social step backward from the Upper East Side (whatever!). The Clinton Hill home located at 299 Dekalb Avenue is probably the wisest real estate decision of any character from the show, as those brownstones now sell for millions. (And just like that, Brooklyn remains cool.)

Miranda and Steve's brownstone from *Sex and the City*, 299 DeKalb Avenue (Fort Greene), August 2021.

When Harry Met Sally (1987)

One of the most romantic movies of all time has a scene at the batting cages located at Coney Island where Harry (Billy Crystal) talks about his mature and modern relationship with Sally (Meg Ryan) with Bruno Kirby (RIP), who plays Jess.

HERE ARE A FEW more Brooklyn-flavored romance films that will warm your heart:

- *Alto* (2015) Slope Fitness (808 Union Street in Park Slope) was one of the locations for the lesbian romance by writer/director Mikki del Monico, starring Brooklynite Annabella Sciorra and *American Idol* season three runner-up Diana DeGarmo.
- *I Hate Valentine's Day* (2009) Nia Vardalos wrote and directed this comedy about a woman who has a strict "five-date limit" until she meets a fellow Brooklyn business owner (played by John Corbett). It was filmed in Windsor Terrace and DUMBO. They had significant chemistry in *My Big Fat Greek Wedding*.
- *It's Complicated* (2009) A Nancy Meyers–directed film starring Meryl Streep and Steve Martin, wherein Streep's character is a bakery owner. Said bakery was built inside the Picnic House in Prospect Park, 40 West Drive.
- *Mr. Wonderful* (1993) Matt Dillon plays a man who wants to find a lover for his ex-wife (Annabella Sciorra) so he can marry Mary-Louise Parker. James Gandolfini appears in an early role. It was filmed partly in Park Slope.

- *Remember Me* (2010) Robert Pattinson (Tyler Hawkins) and Emilie de Ravin (Ally Craig) fall in love pre-9/11 New York. Tyler's mother is played by Lena Olin, and her house is in Brooklyn Heights at 13 Cranberry Street.
- *They Came Together* (2014) Paul Rudd (Joel) and Amy Poehler (Molly) are paired in this spoof (directed by David Wain of *Wet Hot American Summer* fame) on romantic comedies filmed in Brooklyn Heights and Cobble Hill.

CHAPTER 7

INDIES AND AUTEURS

"Please Baby, Please Baby, Please!"

I do have hope, but right now, I'm in financial dire straits. My rent was due October 1. My $500 reimbursement check to the Black Filmmaker Foundation bounced. I got a Con Ed bill of $60. But I do have some money coming in.
—Spike Lee, October 11, 1985

Brooklyn has been a canvas for artists for over two centuries. Its cobbled streets, beaches, brownstones, affordable housing neighborhoods, condominiums, parks, coffee shops, historical buildings and millions of residents live and breathe the past and the present. Brooklyn means young and single. Married with children. Old and settled in your ways. Middle-aged and seeking new adventures. Longtime natives mixed with newcomers seeking to gentrify and change the environment.

Directors, actors, writers and artists have used Brooklyn as a backdrop for decades to celebrate its diversity and help tell its stories. It was the home to early Black lesbian culture in 1920s Coney Island (one of the first places legendary comedian Moms Mabley started her career). Post–World War II saw a boom in artist communes in

Spike Lee with Anthony Ramos in *She's Gotta Have It* (2017). *David Lee/ Netflix.*

Brooklyn Heights, attracting Carson McCullers, Paul Bowles and stripper Gypsy Rose Lee.

Brooklyn has several generations of writers and actors who have used their native and adopted homesteads as the backdrop for their creations.

SPIKE LEE

She's Gotta Have It (1986)

If there were a formal title for "King of Brooklyn Cinema," it would belong to Spike Lee. Shelton Jackson Lee was born to a middle-class family in 1957 who moved from Atlanta to Fort Greene, Brooklyn, when he was young. He is the oldest of four kids, and his middle sister Joie Lee described to the *Los Angeles Times* in 1990 growing up in a family that had an intense interest in the arts and social justice. Though he was smaller than his peers, no one fought Spike Lee. "We lived and breathed [the art]. It wasn't oppressive," according to Joie.

His first feature, *She's Gotta Have It*, was financed for just $175,000, shot in fifteen days in and around the Fort Greene area and would make $8 million (about $20 million in today's dollars). The story of Nola Darling (Tracy Camilla Johns), a Black woman with a strong sex drive who has no shame about it, was a revelation for the time. Juggling three different beaus while living in a gorgeous loft located at the former location of Ferry Bank Restaurant (1 Fulton Street), Nola was unapologetically sensual. Lee's quirky performance as Mars Blackman ("Please baby! Please baby! Please!") brought the comedy audiences to art houses and independent theaters in droves.

DeWanda Wise, Spike Lee and Cleo Anthony in *She's Gotta Have It* (2017). *David Lee/Netflix.*

One would think that a big-time movie company would make him an offer and snap him up. But Spike was opinionated and wanted to make movies about race, politics, sex and culture. (This is *not* a person interested in a buddy cop action-comedy.)

Spike Lee went from a broke film student to an international star in a few short years. He continues to use Brooklyn as a location as often as possible. His projects full of his passion and vitality are a testament to his intelligence, spirit and lifelong affiliation with the arts to promote civic engagement.

40 Acres and a Mule, outside the store at 75 Elliott Place (Fort Greene), July 2021.

He created the 40 Acres and a Mule production company (A Spike Lee Joint!), which you can visit at 75 South Elliott Place to buy his films, books, T-shirts and CDs of his soundtracks. There is usually a bit of a wait, so bring a coffee and make small talk with fellow "Lee Geeks" while posing in front of several works of graffiti devoted to some of his most iconic images.

Lee revisited the character of Nola Darling with a two-season TV adaptation for Netflix in 2017–19, featuring his wife, Tonya Lewis Lee, as executive producer and a writers' room primarily filled with African American women. The show was filmed mainly in Fort Greene, which has become gentrified since 1986 and is now one of the hippest neighborhoods in Brooklyn. The character of Nola (played by DeWanda Wise) juggles three lovers, but this time we also learn more about her experience as an artist. There isn't a "male gaze" about her sexuality, which Lee admitted to RottenTomatoes.com in 2017 made the original production appear dated and judgmental.

> *Oh, how I love* She's Gotta Have It*! A woman gets to enjoy her sexuality. She gets to be gorgeous, Black and makes love enthusiastically and consensually. I had no idea how rare that was. Years later, studying film in college, a professor told us it wasn't just rare. It was a first.*
> —*Kristen Meinzer, co-host,* By the Book, Movie Therapy with Rafer & Kristen, *and culture critic*

Do the Right Thing (1989)

One of Lee's most celebrated films is 1989's *Do the Right Thing*, which takes place in Bedford-Stuyvesant on the hottest day of the summer. Spike Lee stars as Mookie, a young man who works delivering pies from Sal's Pizza. Danny Aiello plays Sal.

Throughout the film, Mookie argues with his girlfriend, attempts to reason with a racist coworker (who happens to be the owner's son) and acts as a peacemaker in his rapidly gentrifying neighborhood.

The film also has a Greek chorus of older Black men (led by late comedian Robin Harris) to lighten the mood. Radio Raheem (Bill Nunn) strolls around with a giant boombox playing "Fight the Power" by Public Enemy to symbolize Black pride. Rosie Perez blazes the screen with an opening sequence that will stay in your mind forever.

The film's central theme is race and racism in American culture. Even though it technically exists in a post–civil rights era, for many people of color, the American dream is not available to them. Even worse is that the justice system actively works to keep them incarcerated and stuck in a poverty cycle.

The thing to remember here is that a little over five months after the release of *Do the Right Thing*, a sleeper hit called *Driving Miss Daisy* landed in movie theaters to rapturous reviews, demonstrating how delicately the issue of racism in America is handled. Taking place between the 1940s and 1970 (during the civil rights movement), it is the story of Miss Daisy (Jessica Tandy, in an Academy Award–winning performance) and her chauffeur (played by Morgan Freeman), who, after decades of him working for her, decides he is a human being deserving of respect and friendship.

In 1990, the Academy Awards featured two nominations for *Do the Right Thing*: Best Supporting Actor for Danny Aiello and Best Screenplay for Spike Lee, with neither one winning. The intense storyline mixed laughter

Site of Sal's Pizzeria, Lexington and Stuyvesant Avenues (Bedford Stuyvesant), August 2021.

with gritty violence and blatant racist words to show how broken our country really was (and still is), which supposedly "scared" many Academy voters.

At the ceremony, actor Kim Basinger went off-script during her presentation. She called out that *Do the Right Thing* deserved a Best Picture nomination over *Driving Miss Daisy*, to tepid applause. Two years later, the L.A. riots would occur over several nights not far from the Dorothy Chandler Pavilion (the site of the Oscars for decades), showing how much America needs to reconcile its racism and how the media can be both a help and a hindrance to accurate communication.

A huge source of conflict in the film is the death of Radio Raheem by the police (who strangle him in a chokehold), which ignites a passion in Mookie to throw a garbage can through the window of Sal's Pizzeria. The entire block turns to mayhem, resulting in Sal's business being destroyed and several arrests of residents. Mookie is not only unrepentant about his actions, but he shows up the next day to demand his week's pay from Sal. Lee noted to the Criterion Channel that in the more than thirty years since the film's release, not one reporter ever asked why the police killed Radio Raheem. They only asked why Mookie threw the garbage can.

The actual location was on Stuyvesant Street between Quincy and Lexington Avenue. You can visit and find some of the most beautiful homes in the city and a vibrant, diverse community with plenty of food options but, sadly, no Sal's Pizza. (It was created on a film set and not based on an actual pizzeria.)

First of all, several of Spike Lee's movies are why I moved to Brooklyn in the early 1990s and why I will never leave, despite traveling the world extensively.

Do the Right Thing blew my mind from the opening dance sequence with Rosie Perez set to the music of Public Enemy. That scene is the piano out of the window. I had never seen anything like that opening and certainly nothing like from a Black film director. It was bold, fearless, visionary. I remember interviewing Spike Lee a few years later, and he was hard on himself, saying the film was technically all wrong. I respectfully disagreed then and do now. It is a brilliant ensemble cast, diverse and gifted, capturing one long day in Brooklyn. And our community's beauty and messiness, all of it.

The movie foreshadowed everything from the Los Angeles rebellion of 1992 to the police murder on camera of George Floyd. It explored

The block on Stuyvesant Avenue where the movie was filmed—Do the Right Thing Way. It is also the site of the Korean Deli in the film. (Bedford Stuyvesant), August 2021.

Above, left: Site of Mother Sister's (Ruby Dee) stoop in *Do the Right Thing*, 161 Stuyvesant (Bedford Stuyvesant), August 2021.

Above, right: Mookie's stoop in *Do the Right Thing* on Stuyvesant Avenue (Bedford Stuyvesant), August 2021.

Opposite, left: Spike Lee's 40 Acres and a Mule store at 75 Elliott Place (Fort Greene), July 2021.

Opposite, right: A mural at 40 Acres and a Mule honoring late members of the cast of *Do the Right Thing*, July 2021.

gentrification, what community means and for whom. I remember gasping and crying at the end of the film, emotionally spent, numb, but glad to see Spike Lee had made this film, and more than ever, as both an artist and activist myself, to be an agent for change.

—Kevin Powell, poet, journalist, filmmaker, civil and human rights activist and biographer of Tupac Shakur

OTHER SPIKE LEE FILMS that have roots in Brooklyn include:
- *Clockers* (1995) Set in pre-gentrified Boerum Hill and Fort Greene, *Clockers* is about drug dealers and a murder mystery to be solved by Detective Rocco Klein (Harvey Keitel).
- *Crooklyn* (1993) Lee's love letter to the 1970s and Brooklyn living (written by his sister Joie Lee) was filmed in Bedford-Stuyvesant and had a soundtrack with some of the best soul music of the decade.
- *He Got Game* (1998) Stars Denzel Washington as a parolee trying to convince his talented son (Ray Allen) to accept a college education at the governor's alma mater versus playing professional basketball right out of high school. It takes place in Coney Island.
- *Inside Man* (2006) Stars Clive Owen, Denzel Washington and Jodie Foster. This story about a bank heist in Manhattan has an opening sequence from Coney Island to the Brooklyn Bridge that is entirely amazing. And the rest of the movie delivers as well!
- *Jungle Fever* (1991) Wesley Snipes and Annabella Sciorra play an interracial couple trying to make their relationship work even

though he is already married. Neither has support from their friends or family. It was partly filmed in Bensonhurst and also stars Samuel L. Jackson, John Turturro, Frank Vincent, Halle Berry and Queen Latifah.

- *Malcolm X* (1992) Denzel Washington stars as the civil rights icon and damn well should have won the Academy Award for it. Also, with Angela Bassett, Delroy Lindo and Debi Mazar.
- *Red Hook Summer* (2012) A boy (Jules Brown) visits a relative (Clarke Peters) in Red Hook for the summer and learns about his uncle's grotesque past.
- *25th Hour* (2002) Montgomery Brogan (Edward Norton) is about to head off to jail for drug dealing and has twenty-four hours to figure out how he got to this place in his life. Nightclub scenes were filmed at Water Street under the Brooklyn Bridge.

Spike Lee is also known around Brooklyn for holding block parties near his Fort Greene home, which was the unofficial gathering spot after the deaths of Prince and Michael Jackson. My friend Martha attended a few of them, and the music was always "off the chain."

DARREN ARONOFSKY

Pi (1997), *Requiem for a Dream* (2000) and *Black Swan* (2010)

Coney Island native Darren Aronofsky grew up in the '70s and '80s, describing to *Brooklyn* magazine in 2015 that life by the famous boardwalk, then in disrepair, was "Lynchian beauty…a beach covered in trash, the irony of a dead amusement park." Perhaps this dystopian look at his surroundings influenced his filmmaking style, often described as "daring" and "jarring." His films include the controversial *Mother!* with Jennifer Lawrence, *The Wrestler* with Mickey Rourke and *Noah* starring Russell Crowe.

In 1998, the Harvard grad borrowed $60,000 from family and acquaintances to fund his first film, *Pi*, about a brilliant mathematician looking to solve his life's problems with numbers. Filmed in black-and-white and partly on the Coney Island Boardwalk (and with no permits), he won Best Director at the Sundance Film Festival and became an indie hit, earning over $3 million at the box office.

Darren Aronofsky,
Odessa International
Film Festival, 2015.
*Creative Commons
Attribution/Andriy Makukha
(Amakuha).*

His follow-up was the bleak and haunting *Requiem for a Dream* starring Jared Leto, Jennifer Connelly, Marlon Wayans and Ellen Burstyn (nominated for a Best Actress Academy Award for her performance), all people in the throes of different kinds of addiction. The adaptation of Brooklyn writer Hubert Selby Jr.'s work was filmed in Brighton Beach and Coney Island at several locations, including the famous Parachute Jump on the boardwalk and the Clam Bar at 1320 Surf Avenue. Mr. Rabinowitz's store at 805 Surf Avenue was created for the film.

The year 2010 brought *Black Swan*, which Aronofsky planned as a companion piece to *The Wrestler* and starred Natalie Portman as a prima ballerina who wishes to lead in *Swan Lake*. Her main competition is Mila Kunis as Lily, with Winona Ryder as the "Dying Swan" who is getting "too old" to perform at a top level. Portman spent a year training for the part, which ultimately won her a Best Actress Academy Award. Her character's apartment was filmed across the street from the Brooklyn Museum in Prospect Heights.

Even a Philadelphian like me is willing to admit that New York is the greatest city in the world. It's vibrant. Alive. Timeless. The more I get to know it, the more I'm captivated by its grandeur, the grandeur most filmmakers seek to emphasize in their most ambitious work. Cinema is lousy with carefree protagonists crossing the Brooklyn Bridge in drop-top and stilettos, eager to bet their future on the City that Never Sleeps. Even the hardscrabble characters of '70s Scorsese pictures walked its glistening avenues and weaved their way through many sights, sounds and cultures.

But not the restless reprobates at the center of Darren Aronofsky's Requiem for a Dream. *Their New York—Brighton Beach alleyways and Coney Island boardwalks—is stifled and claustrophobic. It's a prison, an endless maze of addictions and attractions meant to captivate and consume. Harry, Marion and Tyrone are the titular dreamers, hoping that those alleyways and boardwalks won't be the outer limits of their young lives.*

Even Sara—Ellen Burstyn—gets lost in the shuffle in her Oscar-nominated role. The only hint of open-air, of true, spiritual freedom, is the pier Harry sees in his dreams. He'll never get there, of course. Not in this life. However, the beauty of New York is that it's always ready to start again. It's waiting. Will you be next?

—Rob DiCristino, staff writer for FThisMovie.com

HAL ASHBY

The Landlord (1970)

Hal Ashby spent the first part of his career as a film editor and won an Academy Award for *In the Heat of the Night* in 1967. By 1969, he was looking for a new challenge when his friend, director Norman Jewison, told him about a script about a young, wealthy white man from Long Island who buys a Brooklyn tenement building with plans to gut and renovate, displacing dozens of Black families. Ashby was told starting in the cutting room would prepare him to be a director. When Jewison offered him the opportunity to film *The Landlord*, he "danced frantically around the office. He was finally there," according to Nick Dawson's book *Being Hal Ashby*.

The Landlord is based on a 1966 book by Kristin Hunter and a screenplay by Bill Gunn, both of whom are Black and write viscerally about race relations. On top of overseeing his first film with a very political bent and leaning into white liberal hypocrisy, Ashby married Joan Marshall during the shoot and used the footage in the movie. The marriage did not last very long.

The filming took place in Park Slope at 51 Prospect Street and Flatbush Avenue with Beau Bridges (Hal Ashby's good friend) as the lead. Lee Grant plays his mother (later nominated for an Academy Award for her performance), and the cast of new and veteran actors includes Louis Gossett Jr., Diana Sands and Pearl Bailey. The neighborhood is now one of the most expensive places to live in New York City, and entire sections are preserved as National Landmarks—but in 1970, it was decaying like much of New York City. While being chased up and down Flatbush Avenue, Beau Bridges's character decides to take care of the building and its tenants while having a little romance.

According to Dawson's *Being Hal Ashby*, "Ashby filmed in Brooklyn's then largely African American Park Slope district, where he employed many black crew members and took on many locals as extras." Comedian Charlie Murphy, who was ten years old, plays one of the kids stealing Beau Bridges's tires early in the film.

Left: Beau Bridges in *The Landlord* (1970). *AF Archive/Alamy Stock Photo.*

Right: *The Landlord* exterior at 51 Prospect Place (Park Slope), April 2021.

In May 1970, the box office disappointment was blamed on being ahead of its time in talks about race, the gentrification of inner cities and interracial relationships. The marketing was geared toward a sex comedy, but that misses the point of the real racial and sexual politics, which would be explored more in the decades to come by directors as daring as Spike Lee.

Beau Bridges would later tell the *New York Times* in 2007, "It's kind of an imperfect film because it was Hal's first, and he kind of honed his craft as he went along." Ashby died in 1988.

The Landlord eventually found an audience on home video and is considered one of Ashby's finest works. Prominently featured in Hal Ashby film festivals and taught in film schools worldwide, it is now considered a cult classic. (His career would skyrocket with the following year's release of *Harold and Maude*.)

> *I was still living in Hartford, Connecticut, when I first saw the film, and I barely gave it a second thought since all I knew firsthand about Brooklyn came from mid-1960s summer visits to relatives living in Fort Hamilton.*
>
> *The revelations came when I saw the movie in the 1990s when I lived in Prospect Heights, only a few blocks from where it was filmed. I knew the Slope well enough to recognize most if not all of the exterior locations. Even though the prism of time converted that Prospect Park region into a Promised Land for the well-to-do, I could perceive not so much a "ghetto" vibe to the movie's setting as a working-class neighborhood like the one I grew up in central Connecticut. These days, Hartford now looks more like what the movie's Park Slope looked like then.*
>
> *—Gene Seymour, former film critic at* Newsday *and contributor to such publications as* The Nation, CNN.com *and the* Washington Post

PAUL AUSTER

Smoke and *Blue in the Face* (1995)

Writer Paul Auster is a Brooklyn institution with several bestsellers since his first novel, *The New York Trilogy*, came out in 1987. His work is translated into more than forty languages, and it is not unusual to find a flyer in a Park Slope coffee shop from a traveler from Berlin wishing to meet him. He used to have a reputation for being agreeable to these things, but it soon became unmanageable.

In the mid-1990s, he wrote a few screenplays based on a short story for the *New York Times* in 1990, "Auggie Wren's Christmas Story," which included an incredible amount of improvisation and an open invitation for performers who wanted to join in the fun, including Forest Whitaker, Lou Reed, Harvey Keitel, Stockard Channing, William Hurt and Giancarlo Esposito. *Smoke*, his first film, was released in June 1995, featuring a cast of likable characters who hang around and trade stories in and around a Brooklyn smoke shop. Directed by Wayne Wang, it became an indie hit with several festivals worldwide. (MTV honored the film by giving it an award at the 1996 MTV Awards for the "Ham and Cheese Sandwich!")

Blue in the Face arrived in theaters in October 1995 and centers more on the romances between the customers and staff at the smoke shop, with guest appearances by Madonna, Michael J. Fox, Roseanne Barr and Mira Sorvino. It was filmed in ten-minute sequences with no interruptions. The director held a sign saying "boring" off-camera if the actors were sluggish. Both are considered classics of '90s-era Brooklyn filmmaking.

Location for *Smoke* and *Blue in the Face*, Prospect Park West and 16th Street (Windsor Terrace), May 2022.

The central location, the Brooklyn Cigar Company, remains as the charming-looking Betty Bakery at 211 Prospect Park West in Windsor Terrace, right across the street from Farrells Bar (a Brooklyn institution). This location is the same corner referred to as "3rd Street and 7th Avenue" in *Smoke*, where Harvey Keitel's character takes a photo at 8:00 a.m. every day for several years.

Also, in *Smoke*, Harvey Keitel (Auggie) and Stockard Channing (Ruby) try to rescue their daughter Felicity from

The original *Smoke* shop location is now Betty Bakery at 211 Prospect Park West (Windsor Terrace), June 2022. The sign painter is Liv Novotny (@Liv.Handpaints).

addiction issues (played by Ashley Judd). The outside shots of her apartment are in a pre-gentrified Williamsburg at 412 Bedford Avenue. The spot where William Hurt (Paul) is saved by Rashid (Harold Perrineau) from being hit by a truck is located at 72 7th Avenue (at Berkeley Street) in Park Slope.

One of the oldest bars in Brooklyn is located at 138 Bergen Street in Boerum Hill (the Brooklyn Inn) and is used as a scene where Auggie and Paul enjoy a drink. It's been open since 1885 and is supposedly haunted. The last location of *Smoke* is Auggie chasing a thief ostensibly outside his store, but it was filmed at 300 Court Street in Carroll Gardens.

NOAH BAUMBACH

Mr. Jealousy (1997), *The Squid and the Whale* (2005) and *Marriage Story* (2019)

These days, Park Slope is a setting for middle- and upper-middle-class characters who like urban living and are uninterested in life in the suburbs. (We call Manhattan "the city" and enjoy our quiet and space here.) In the 1970s, it was mainly filled with blue-collar families, civil servants and teachers. The brownstones that would eventually sell for millions were filled with multiple generations of family members and were part of the grittiness that existed in New York City in the "Me Decade."

In 1997, Park Slope was the background for Noah Baumbach's romantic comedy follow-up to 1995's *Kicking and Screaming*, called *Mr. Jealousy*. The neighborhood was going through a makeover with upper-middle-class to wealthy people buying brownstones and creating a need for fancy restaurants and shops. The film stars '90s "cool indie kids" Eric Stoltz, Annabella Sciorra and Marianne Jean-Baptiste and mainly uses Prospect Park West as a background for the romantic banter between Stoltz and Sciorra. The film is notable for Baumbach's tortured male leads who wear their hearts on their sleeves, and the director narrates the story of a man who is so jealous of his girlfriend's ex-boyfriend that he infiltrates

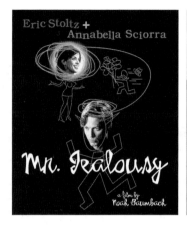
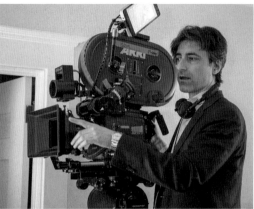

Left: *Mr. Jealousy* DVD & Blue-Ray cover. *MVD Entertainment Group.*

Right: Noah Baumbach's *Marriage Story*, 2019. *Wilson Webb/Netflix.*

his therapy group. Director Peter Bogdanovich plays the group therapy counselor.

The Squid and the Whale is a fictionalized account of Baumbach's parents' separation in the 1970s. The film stars Jeff Daniels and Laura Linney, with most of the action taking place in their brownstone located at 167 6th Avenue. It was the first film he had directed in eight years, and it was vital for him to use the location of his childhood. He said at the New York Film Festival that year, "It's meaningful to me to shoot on a street that I walked as a kid. It brings something out in me." The scenes with Jeff Daniels desperately searching for parking and his eventual landing in Ditmas Park, considered the scary neighborhood "on the other side of the park," ring with audiences today. Ditmas Park became an economically desirous neighborhood with many restaurants and shopping to rival Park Slope by the film's release.

Marriage Story is about Broadway playwright Charlie Barber (played by Adam Driver) divorcing his actress wife, Nicole Barber (Scarlett Johansson). The latter wants to live in Los Angeles and raise their son bicoastally. By the time of this film, Park Slope was home to many celebrities and wealthy folks who think nothing of buying a $5 million brownstone to gut and rebuild from scratch.

Baumbach said he mined a bit from his own life and his friend's divorce experiences for his script. He also cites the 1978 film *Invasion of the Body Snatchers*, which scared him as a child, as an influence. "The idea that someone you love and trust changing into another person," he told *Esquire* magazine in 2019. "The concept of it just scared me so much."

Above, left: The Berkman brownstone for *The Squid and the Whale*, 167 7th Avenue (Park Slope), March 2021.

Above, top right: Scarlett Johansson (Nicole Barber) and Adam Driver (Charlie Barber) in *Marriage Story*, 2019. *Netflix*.

Above, bottom right: Pino's La Forchetta Pizza (*Marriage Story*) at 181 7th Avenue (Park Slope), March 2021.

Left: Greta Gerwig and Noah Baumbauch at the New York premiere of *Marriage Story*, November, 10, 2019, hosted by Netflix at the Paris Theater. *Marion Curtis/Netflix*.

The film was streamed over Netflix in December 2019 and earned critical praise for the whole cast, which includes Ray Liotta, Julie Hagerty and Laura Dern, who won an Academy Award for Best Supporting Actress as lawyer Nora Fanshaw. The movie was also nominated for Best Picture, Best Actress

(Johannsson), Best Actor (Driver), Best Original Score (Randy Newman) and Best Screenplay (Baumbach).

Several locations in Park Slope were used to demonstrate their married life in Brooklyn, including 7th Avenue between 2nd and 3rd Streets, with a local pizza parlor and laundromat as the settings. (Locals say "Kylo Ren" was amiable and accommodating for Star Wars fans looking for autographs.) Next to that location is Pino's Pizzeria, where the family enjoys a pie. (The pizza is quite good, by the way!)

OTHER NOAH BAUMBACH FILMS that are shot in Brooklyn include:
- *Frances Ha* (2012) The East Broadway F-train stop is featured in a vital scene about a big-dream dancer.
- *Mistress America* (2015) Starring his partner, actor/writer/director Greta Gerwig, this film uses Park Slope as a backdrop for several key scenes.

RADHA BLANK

The Forty-Year-Old Version (2020)

Williamsburg's Radha Blank is a talented creator who gained a following after her film *The Forty-Year-Old Version* was shown at the 2020 Sundance Film Festival, winning the U.S. Dramatic Competition Directing Award. With producing help from actor/producer Lena Waithe, Blank wrote, acted in, produced and directed the story of a formerly successful playwright turned

Radha Blank directing *The Forty-Year-Old Version. Jeong Park/Netflix ©2020.*

high school acting teacher who dreams of a rap career in her forties. Netflix picked up the film, which currently has a 98 percent score on *Rotten Tomatoes*. She has a few hip-hop scenes that take place in Brownsville.

Born in Williamsburg, Blank told the Sundance Institute in 2017 (where she won the annual screenwriting competition) that she developed her hip-hop comedy as RadhaMUSprime to be vulnerable and express herself. The film features her brother Ravi Blank as her movie sibling and is dedicated to her mother, Carol Blank, a visual artist who passed away in 2013.

Some of her songs on the soundtrack include "Poverty Porn" (a parody about musicals that glorify gentrification throughout New York City), "This Some Bull***," "Harlem Ave" and "F.Y.O.V.," where the audience is encouraged to "Find Your Own Vision." From "Poverty Porn": "You regular blacks are such a yawn/Yo, if I wanna get on/Better write me some poverty porn!"

Blank told the *New York Times* in 2022 that she was working on her next project while walking around all the boroughs enjoying "subway theater"—listening in on the conversations around her. "I'm not an outsider. I see myself as the people I'm writing about."

REBECCA HALL

Passing (2021)

Actor, writer, producer and director Rebecca Hall is the product of a British father (director Peter Hall) and American mother (opera singer Maria Ewing) of African American and Dutch ancestry. Hall produced, directed and adapted the screenplay for the 1929 novel *Passing* as her feature film debut. The film tells the story of two Black women, Irene Redfield (Tessa Thompson) and Clare Kendry (Ruth Negga), who can "pass" as white but choose to live on opposite sides of the color line during the height of the Harlem Renaissance in the 1920s. It was partly filmed in Brooklyn Heights and at the Boathouse and Audubon in Prospect Park. The independent production was picked up by Netflix, which helped the film reach an international audience, and it received raves from viewers and critics.

Passing (left to right), Tessa Thompson, Ruth Negga and director Rebecca Hall at the Prospect Park Boathouse and Audubon, 2021. *Emily V. Aragones/Netflix.*

Hall spent ten years bringing the book to life while building on a successful acting career in projects as varied as *Iron Man 3* to *The Town* and *Christine*, in which she played the part of real-life TV anchor Christine Chubbuck, who died by suicide while on the air in 1974. She told the *New York Times* in 2021 that her first read of *Passing* felt like a "gut punch" and that she had to figure out a way to make it properly. She and her producing

Top: Prospect Park Boathouse and Audubon (indoors, summer 2021).

Bottom: André Holland and director Rebecca Hall in 2021's *Passing. Emily V. Aragones/Netflix.*

partner, Margot Hand, decided it had to be shot in black-and-white, in a 4:3 aspect ratio, and it had to have a Black cast, which Hall said gave it all a "lost noir film" look. According to David Rooney of the *Hollywood Reporter* in 2021, "Whether this is a one-time passion project or the beginnings of an ongoing move from acting into directing or her career focus, Hall has crafted a work that's thoughtful, provocative, and emotionally resonant."

LESLIE HARRIS

Just Another Girl on the I.R.T. (1992)

In 1992, Leslie Harris became the first African American woman to win a special jury prize at the Sundance Film Festival for her debut *Just Another Girl on the I.R.T.* The story revolves around a teen girl who lives in the projects of Downtown Brooklyn and is a bright high school student who dreams of going to college when an unexpected pregnancy changes her life. It was one of the first films centered on a teenage Black girl (Chantel Mitchell, played by Ariyan A. Johnson). Harris, through several grants, raised the $100,000 needed to film the story in just seventeen days, including on the IRT (which stands for Interborough Rapid Transit) Lexington Street subway. One of my friends remarked how excited she was to see "a girl who looked like me breaking through the fourth wall to talk to the audience. That has never happened before or since!"

Distributed by Miramax and earning over $400,000 at the box office, it is now considered a classic of '90s independent cinema. However, Harris has not been able to secure financing for any feature films since then and instead taught filmmaking and screenwriting at the New York University Tisch School of the Arts. Her dream is to make a sequel to let fans know what happened to Chantel. During a twentieth anniversary screening at the 92nd Street Y in New York City, she said to the audience, "Let's not forget the contributions of Black women in the history of the indie film world." You can see Chantel's home at 224 York Street.

CHAPTER 8

LOCATION SHOOTING IN BROOKLYN

Shooting in Brooklyn is like opening a time capsule. Nothing has changed.
Everything looks like it did in the '80s.
—*an inaccurate Freddie Prinze Jr.*

One of the perks of living in Brooklyn is the sheer number of movies, music videos and TV shows filmed here, with dozens of productions happening at the same time most of the year. (*Law & Order* and all its iterations have been spotted in all areas of Brooklyn for going on three decades now.) To film anywhere in New York City, you need a permit through the Mayor's Office of Media Management. Most city locations are accessible, but some do have a cost associated with the extra work for security, proof of liability insurance and maintaining the integrity of the space (i.e., making sure the place is not harmed by filming).

Public spaces often used in Brooklyn are Prospect Park, Brooklyn Bridge and Fort Greene Park, and you need to obtain permission to film if you are not a news crew. Some accommodations are meant for low-budget productions and student filmmakers, but even they can still be too pricey for most to handle.

Some productions avoid this by eschewing the whole process and sneaking in shoots where they feel lucky enough to get away with it. (I am not recommending that, by the way!) Spike Lee did this for *She's Gotta Have It* in his beloved Fort Greene, and Darren Aronofsky's *Pi* shot on Coney Island. They admit their debut efforts required ducking the permits and

Rachel Weisz shooting *Dead Ringers* on 5th Street between 8th Avenue and Prospect Park West in Park Slope, December 2021.

filming "on the fly." Howard Stern's movie *Private Parts* was noticed filming a quick shot of the star running across St. John's Street in Park Slope. (Maybe Stern wanted to avoid his fans showing up to yell "Baba Booey!") His six-foot-five-inch lanky frame and big, curly mop of hair stood out for the bystanders.

Director Richard Schenkman partnered with actor and writer Jon Cryer in 1998 for the independent film *Went to Coney Island on a Mission from God… Be Back by Five* and found shooting on location both a delight and filled with its hazards. "You can achieve such stupendous production value when you go and shoot on location; it's why filmmakers have done it since the very first days of motion picture production," he told me.

Typically, if you want to shoot in New York City, you must place a neon-colored sign at least forty-eight hours in advance showing the day, date and time of shooting with the project name available. The poster gives residents time to prepare and find another place to park if they do not have a driveway. I have personally witnessed people hired to live out of a car for a few days to protect spaces on the street for (sometimes) vintage cars, trailers, bathrooms, trucks full of gear and catering. The return of Christopher Meloni's character Elliot Stabler to *Law & Order* caused such a commotion in Park

Signage for Prospect Park West location for *Dead Ringers* (Park Slope), December 2021.

15th Street film set (Windsor Terrace) for Phoebe Robinson (of *2 Dope Queens* fame) and her newest show, *Everything's Trash*, April 2022.

Slope (a neighborhood very used to the franchise taping) that pictures of his derriere trended on Twitter!

I asked editor Mary Lukasiewicz, who has worked on several Academy Award–nominated productions, including *Dune, Arrival* and *Blade Runner 2049*, what goes into deciding to film on location. She said it was down to "budget, vision, time and tax breaks." Cities with significant tax breaks include New York, Toronto and Montreal, where consistent filming will be. Georgia has become very friendly to entertainment production for the last few years, being home for everything from the series *Ozark* to *Coming 2 America*.

Why is Brooklyn so valuable a location? According to Lukasiewicz, "There is something different about a city where everybody is smashed together in such a small amount of space, which adds drama, and all good movies have drama. You can almost film a person washing their car on the street, and you don't need to write anything around it. There is inherent tension and juiciness in the city's vibrancy and how everyone has to get along."

If you ever spend a day on a film set (I worked as an extra on several in college), you quickly learn that making films is mastering the art of waiting.

They are waiting for the weather to clear, actors to leave their trailers, the crew to set up lights, the sound person to approve the recording or stay after hours for a business to close to shoot interiors late into the night.

The setups can take days, while the actual filming occurs in minutes. It's not uncommon to see crew members (when they are not talking endlessly on their phones) playing board games or standing around chatting to pass the time. Some are tasked with keeping the sets "clear" with no bystanders or people walking into their shot. You can spot them by their headsets, clipboards and sometimes-gruff manners, asking you to leave, cross the street or wait until they are done. A seasoned New Yorker knows how to walk looking unperturbed while sneaking a glance to see if someone *really* famous is on the set.

"New York City has such a thriving production community," Schenkman told me. "A couple of the best film schools in the nation are located in NYC, so there is always a crop of young people willing to work hard for a break into the film business." I asked him whether there are any drawbacks to filming on location. He answered that some neighborhoods and places are "over-shot," meaning the residents may complain about the number of productions happening on their block. This means creators must hold back from shooting there, as permits may be harder to come by. This affects the independent filmmaker much more than the bigger studios.

Longtime Park Slope resident Paul Bernstein, who lived on St. John's Street from 1979 to 2019, clued me in on what it is like to have film crews invade the neighborhood, with crew members who range in temperament from frazzled and hurried to outright rude and dictatorial. It's not huge news to say that so much time is needed for just a few minutes of the film, and most of what is shot is discarded. You can eat from the catering trucks and enjoy the spectacle if you are lucky. If not, bright lights can shine into your home all night.

To have a crew film in your home/place of residence can be a nice side hustle, but it comes with its drawbacks. You need to understand that dozens of people will be in and out of your home, moving and rearranging furniture (and not remembering where to put things back), annoying your neighbors and (in the case of one person who told me they wanted anonymity) the possibility of people sneaking cigarettes even though they promised a smoke-free atmosphere. The amount you are paid depends on the size of the budget, and you need to be aware of certain risks to this arrangement.

Bernstein told me the story about when he first lived in Park Slope in 1979 and was paid for using his apartment in the film *The Squeeze* starring Karen

Jon Cryer and Richard Schenkman (1998) in *Went to Coney Island on a Mission from God...Be Back by Five*. *Photo by Tom Legoff*.

Black. His abode served as the home for Black's character, and the Italian crew paid him a $150 stipend (about $500 in today's dollars). Someone on the set was homesick and made several long-distance calls to Italy. Bernstein was stuck with a phone bill of $700, equivalent to over $2,300 today!

Consider several things if you want to investigate having your home listed as a film location. The fee (anywhere from $500 to $5,000 per day) depends on the production size and how many days are needed. You need to understand that the bigger the budget, the bigger the headache for your neighbors, who may not appreciate having their driveways blocked by dressing rooms, makeup stations and massive trailers (called "basecamp" by the crew).

The chance of having your home damaged during filming is high, and there are plenty of stories of crews laying down cables, building tracks for cameras, moving (replacing furniture) and scratching up floors. Moving furniture can become damaged by hitting it against walls. Even if solely your front door is being used as a location (such as the final scene in Tom Cruise's *War of the Worlds* with a Carroll Street home standing in for Boston), it will require dozens of crew members inside and outside your home.

Film gear for *Dead Ringers*, a 2022 production, at Prospect Park West at 4th Street in Park Slope, December 2021.

Period films can be an unusual delight, as for the folks who lived on Carroll Street in the early 1990s and witnessed Daniel Day-Lewis walk around the block toward Prospect Park on a horse in Gilded Age gear for Martin Scorsese's *Age of Innocence*. It was a big deal for locals to watch the cast, including Michelle Pfeiffer and Winona Ryder, come and go from Congregation Beth Elohim (274 Garfield Place) as a changing/staging area.

When I posted in the "Park Slope Together" Facebook group about what films people witnessed being shot, Maureen Rice told me she was there when *Dog Day Afternoon* was filmed in Windsor Terrace. It opened her eyes to how "tedious" filmmaking can be. The infamous scene of Al Pacino yelling "Attica!" to the gathered crowd took three whole days to film.

The owners of Slope Fitness in Park Slope were shocked that filming for even a low-budget/indie film *(Alto*, a 2015 lesbian romance starring former *American Idol* runner-up Diana DeGarmo and Brooklyn native Annabella Sciorra) can take up several hours.

Richard Schenkman found out when attempting to set up a shot on the F train subway to Coney Island that the City of New York would not give them a permit, as a previous film had set a fire on a station platform. So, they decided to "steal" the scene by setting up the sequence on the fly. A transit officer waved to them not to stop them but to let them know the F train would run on another platform. "Either he hadn't noticed the camera, or he simply didn't care. We got the whole sequence using only available light, and it looks absolutely beautiful," he adds.

BookCourt, located between Pacific and Dean Streets, famously never closed during any filming (including Larry David's *Curb Your Enthusiasm*). It was one of Brooklyn's best (and most missed!) bookstores. They broke this rule only once—for Julia Roberts's film *Eat Pray Love*. The superstar working on one of the most anticipated movies of 2010 made Carroll Gardens and Cobble Hill all aflutter.

The chance to meet a famous star of a big franchise working on an independent film happened in Park Slope when Adam Driver (*Star Wars*'s Kylo Ren) appeared in *Marriage Story*. Kim Gougenheim recalled her elementary school–aged daughter was "obsessed" with him at the time, as most of her schoolmates were, when he appeared right across the street at her local laundromat. Driver was kind enough to shake hands and take pictures with all. Her daughter spent the rest of the day on her stoop "staring at his trailer."

For decades, the neighborhood of DUMBO was used as a generic "bad/dangerous" location for many films. According to Lee Solomon (from the Park Slope Facebook group), who worked in movies for many years, "the early morning shots of NYC with the sun on Manhattan buildings were a big draw for filmmakers." However, this meant setting up all night in the deserted area. Sometimes the police would be assigned to protect the crew. Nowadays, the location is one of New York's most expensive and represents a chic atmosphere.

Al Pacino, Martin Scorsese and cinematographer Rodrigo Prieto in *The Irishman*, 2019. *Niko Tavernise/Netflix.*

Similarly, shooting in Coney Island in 1998 proved to be a challenge for the crew of *Went to Coney Island* because the neighborhood and boardwalk were being renovated. Originally under the boardwalk was "grotty," according to director Schenkman, but it was soon blocked off and fenced in for cleaning and repairs. He and his cast begged a construction crew to give them a small space to rehearse and film.

The sheer volume of creators, writers, directors, actors and crew based in New York City can help Brooklyn serve as the actual location for films set in cities. Martin Scorsese utilized a few areas in Brooklyn to take the place of Philadelphia for his 2019 three-hour-and-thirty-minute opus *The Irishman* for Netflix, about hitman Frank Sheeran (played by Robert DeNiro) and his crime life with Jimmy Hoffa (Al Pacino) and Joe Pesci, who came out of acting retirement to play mobster Russell Bufalino. The budget of $160 million and the ten Academy Award nominations caught the attention of Hollywood, which had wondered if the streaming platform could provide high-quality content. To be clear, Scorsese (rightfully) demanded in-theater screenings of *The Irishman* first. The result is a beautiful film that artfully uses "de-aging" techniques just recently available for special effects to tell an unsavory true crime story taking place over several decades in the most honest way possible.

The "Iconic Hicks Street Homes," 146 and 148 Hicks Street (Brooklyn Heights), used in *Burn After Reading*, March 2022.

The Andrea Doria Social Club (used in *The Irishman*) was filmed in Carroll Gardens at 268 Smith Street, and the area by the Brooklyn Queens Expressway by the Gowanus Canal was used for a chase scene. Russell tells Frank that there is a "change in plan" at the Colandrea New Corner Restaurant at 7201 8th Avenue in Dyker Heights (a place famous for over-the-top Christmas light displays in December). The Colandrea family told the *Brooklyn Reporter* that it was the first time they allowed a film crew inside their business, which opened in 1936. Scorsese, Pesci and DeNiro were friendly and approachable. Sadly, the restaurant went out of business in 2020 due to the COVID pandemic. More film locations for *The Irishman* are listed in chapter 9.

Burn After Reading from Joel Coen and Ethan Coen is primarily based in the Washington, D.C. area (near CIA headquarters). Instead, several Brooklyn Heights locations were used in its place, according to BrooklynHeightsBlog. com, including the "Iconic 1826 Hicks Street Homes" at 146 and 148 Hicks Street and the Van Sickel salon at 34 Middagh Street. In appreciation for the area's welcome, the Coen brothers were reported to give $10,000 to several local organizations.

RECENT FILMING

While getting this book together, I spied a production sheet that said *Larry's Diner* was to be filmed in Park Slope, but it was the Amazon Prime update of *Dead Ringers*. The original was a 1988 David Cronenberg movie starring Jeremy Irons as a pair of twin gynecologists competing over a woman. In this version, Rachel Weisz plays the Mantle twins, who are doctors looking to change how all women give birth starting in New York City. Her crew did not seem to appreciate my sneaking around to get the shot, but an author's life can be treacherous!

A film crew setting up on 5th Street in Park Slope for *Dead Ringers*, December 2021.

Phoebe Robinson being filmed on 15th Street in Windsor Terrace for *Everything's Trash*, May 2022.

"Lucy and Desi" Honeywagons on the *Dead Ringers* set in Park Slope, December 2021.

Everything's Trash stars Phoebe Robinson (*2 Dope Queens*) as a podcaster with a chaotic life in Brooklyn. The adaptation of her book *Everything's Trash, But It's Okay* will be seen on Freeform. I caught some of their filming on 15th Street in Brooklyn. No one gave me the evil eye there.

Haddad's Honeywagons are on-set bathrooms labeled in honor of Lucille Ball and Desi Arnaz of *I Love Lucy* fame. If you see the Honeywagons on the street, know they are just for the cast and crew of production!

CHAPTER 9

BROOKLYN MOVIES
BY NEIGHBORHOOD

I've been stranded in the combat zone. I walked through Bedford Stuy alone.
—Billy Joel "You May Be Right"

There are dozens of neighborhoods in Brooklyn that feature everything from stoop living to beachcombing and shopping galore. You can say you are "from" Brooklyn as soon as you move here, unlike some less-than-newcomer-friendly places (looking at you, Washington and Maine!). Each area has its history and flavor, with some relatively unchanged over the years and others with a drastically different population than the previous generation.

Brooklyn offers so many options for showing just about any era of American history, from the Civil War to the present day, and is the site for countless TV and movie filming. In compiling this list, I aimed to be as accurate as possible and provide the actual location in the neighborhood featured. Some—especially independent productions done with a bare-bones crew that often works "on the fly"—are unknown for street name or number. Still, they should give you an idea of the breadth of difference and diversity this borough offers.

The Joker Art on Smith Street, May 2022.

BAY RIDGE

Right by the Verrazzano-Narrows Bridge is a neighborhood famous for being "old-school Italian" and blue collar for decades. It is now home to vibrant Chinese, Russian and Muslim communities. The following productions were filmed there:

- *City Hall* (1996) John Cusack and Al Pacino encounter New York City politics in this forgotten '90s thriller that features the Belt Parkway where Frank Anselmo (Danny Aiello) talks to his wife before (spoiler) he dies by suicide.
- *The French Connection* (1971) One of the best car chases of all time takes place on Stillwell Avenue at Bay 50th to 62nd Street.
- *Goodfellas* (1990) Tommy (Joe Pesci) is set up to be killed by the mob at Five 80th Street (at Shore Road—right by Tony Manero's house!).
- *The Kitchen* (2019) This comedy stars Melissa McCarthy, Elisabeth Moss and Tiffany Haddish. Filming includes Nunzio & Lucy Hair Stylists at 9249 Fourth Avenue (serving as Manhattan's Hell's Kitchen) and the 6920 3rd Avenue building as the Galaxy Diner.

Fort Wadsworth Verrazzano-Narrows Bridge. *Creative Commons Attribution/MTKirk, 2019.*

- *Saturday Night Fever* (1977) This film made Bay Ridge famous worldwide. Tony Manero's house is at 221 79th Street (Bay Ridge), 2001 Odyssey Disco is at 802 64th Street and Phillips Dance Studio is at 1301 West 7th Street.
- *Spider-Man 2* (2004) Baby-faced Tobey Maguire stars in his second film about the webbed teenage hero who fights Doc Ock, played by Alfred Molina.

BEDFORD STUYVESANT

Long known as a place for the Black community to thrive, "Bed Stuy" is located around Flatbush and Atlantic Avenues and is one of the growing gentrified Brooklyn areas but still maintains its urbanite charm.

- *Crooklyn* (1994) Spike Lee's darkly funny look at his childhood in 1970s Brooklyn.
- *Do the Right Thing* (1989) The entire film takes place on Stuyvesant Avenue between Quincy and Lexington Avenues.
- *The French Connection* (1971) The Gene Hackman classic was partly filmed at Ellery Street.

Do the Right Thing Way, Stuyvesant Street between Quincy and Lexington. (Bedford Stuyvesant), August 2022.

- *Motherless Brooklyn* (2019) Edward Norton (who directed this film) fought to save the location of the Jacob Dangler House (a 120-year-old mansion used in the movie) on 441 Willoughby Avenue, but it was torn down to create more condos in the summer of 2022.
- *Newlyweeds* (2013) Described on IMDb.com as "a match made in stoner heaven" by writer and director Shaka King (*Judas & the Black Messiah*).
- *Notorious* (2009) The biopic about the life of Christopher "Biggie" Wallace (Jamal Woolard).

BENSONHURST

In the early part of the twentieth century, this neighborhood was home to Italian and Jewish communities. Placed between 65th Street and Avenue P and the Bay Parkway, it now contains its own Chinatown and several other nationalities serving Brooklyn's long history of adapting to new immigrant groups.

- *Angie* (1994) Geena Davis plays a single pregnant woman dreaming of a better life.
- *Goodfellas* (1990) Oriental Manor (site of Karen and Henry's wedding) is at 1818 86th Street.
- *Jungle Fever* (1991) Spike Lee's less than optimistic look at interracial relationships.
- *Out for Justice* (1991) For this Steven Seagal "beat 'em up and shoot 'em up" movie about a Brooklyn detective with a vendetta, filming took place on 17th and 18th Avenues.
- *Saturday Night Fever* (1977) 86th Street (strut!) and Lenny's Pizza, 1969 86th Street.
- *Spike of Bensonhurst* (1988) Sasha Mitchell (of '90s TV staple *Step by Step* fame) plays a local kid who is scared out of his neighborhood by the mob.

BOERUM HILL

Lying in a small patch of streets between Carroll Gardens and Gowanus, this neighborhood was in severe decline until the 1990s and now is home to middle- and upper-middle-class families looking for houses not as ornate as those found in other brownstone-heavy areas.

- *Annie Hall* (1977) The site of Steven's Famous Clam Bar is at 515 Atlantic Avenue.
- *Clockers* (1995) The Gowanus Housing Projects at 211 Hoyt Street was the setting for several scenes. Spike Lee directed this Richard Price story about teens who sell drugs and their bosses in Brooklyn.

BRIGHTON BEACH

A beach-based community was an early place for eastern European Jews and is now a heavily Russian neighborhood with dozens of vodka bars. Located next to Coney Island, it can often look like a substitute for 1940s pre– and post–World War II America.

- *Brighton Beach Memoirs* (1986) A fictional account of playwright Neil Simon's childhood in pre–World War II Brooklyn, starring Jonathan Silverman as Eugene Morris Jerome
- *Little Odessa* (1994) James Gray wrote and directed this story about a Russian immigrant community in the early 1990s, starring Tim Roth and Edward Furlong.
- *Lord of War* (2005) Nicolas Cage plays an amoral arms dealer with Ethan Hawke, Jared Leto and Bridget Moynihan.
- *Moscow on the Hudson* (1984) Robin Williams is a Russian musician (and learned to speak Russian for the part!) who decides to defect to America.
- *Requiem for a Dream* (2000) A brilliant and utterly joyless film that uses Brighton Beach as a background. Sara's (Ellen Burstyn's) apartment is at 3152 Brighton 6th Street at Ocean View.
- *Two Lovers* (2006) A romance and drama about two lovers, Gwyneth Paltrow and Joaquin Phoenix.

BROOKLYN HEIGHTS

The jewel by the Brooklyn Bridge, this neighborhood has been home to dozens of artists, writers, actors and poets, including Truman Capote, Marilyn Monroe, Carson McCullers and Arthur Miller. With names like

The Sentinel corner, 10 Montague Terrace (Brooklyn Heights), September 2021.

Cranberry and Orange Streets, there are brownstones and cobble streets aplenty here and some of the most beautiful homes featured in movies.

- *The Age of Innocence* (1993) A beautiful and romantic film with one of its many brownstones located at 32 Remsen Street (Brooklyn Heights).
- *Bridge of Spies* (2015) Often, old-timey New York City subways are filmed at the New York Transit Museum at 99 Schermerhorn Street, such as in this film.
- *Burn After Reading* (2008) Joel and Ethan Cohen used many locations in Brooklyn Heights, including 34 Middagh Street for Van Sickel Salon (in place of Washington, D.C.) and the "Iconic 1826 Hicks Street Homes" at 146 and 148 Hicks Street.
- *The Godfather* (1972) Luca Brasi (Lenny Montana) was made to "sleep with the fishes" at what is called the Hotel St. George at 100 Henry Street.
- *Midnight Run* (1988) Robert DeNiro starts his journey as a bounty hunter, taking Charles Grodin cross country. He begins at 16 Remsen Street (Grodin's apartment).
- *Moonstruck* (1987) One of the most enjoyable films of the 1980s with locations at 19 Cranberry Street and the Cammareri Bakery at 502 Henry Street.

- *Motherless Brooklyn* (2019) Edward Norton wrote and directed the Jonathan Lethem film, with part of it taking place at Henry Street between Orange and Pineapple Streets.
- *Passing* (2021) Rebecca Hall's debut film was partly shot at the Center for Brooklyn History (128 Pierrepont Street) in place of 1920s Harlem
- *Prizzi's Honor* (1985) The first wedding scene where Kathleen Turner and Jack Nicholson's characters (both contract killers) meet is at the Church of St. Ann at Montague and Clinton Streets. Nicholson's character lives at 57 Montague Street.
- *The Sentinel* (1977) The classic "model buys a scary townhouse horror film" starring Cristina Raines, with her apartment building located at 10 Montague Terrace.
- *Taxi Driver* (1975) Robert DeNiro's Travis Bickle buys guns at 87 Columbia Heights, and his last scene was filmed at Cadman Plaza West near the Park Plaza Diner.
- *Three Days of the Condor* (1975) An excellent spy flick that stars Robert Redford and Faye Dunaway, with locations at Cranberry between Willow and Columbia Heights.
- *The Verdict* (1982) One of Paul Newman's best performances, directed by Sidney Lumet and co-starring Charlotte Rampling, Jack Warden and James Mason. The "Boston" home of Dr. Gruber (Lewis J. Stadlen) was located at 151 Willow Street and was also the former home of the playwright Arthur Miller. Dr. Gruber's office was filmed at 18 Cranberry Street (across the street from the Moonstruck house), and Judge Hoyle's (Milo O'Shea) office was at 20 Willow Street.
- *Winter's Tale* (2014) Colin Farrell plays a burglar who falls in love in this period piece. Filmed partly on Hicks Street.

BROWNSVILLE

The neighborhood that begat Mike Tyson was in the early part of the twentieth century inhabited mainly by a Jewish population and was the home turf of the gang Murder Incorporated before the African American migration from the South in the 1960s.

- *The Forty-Year-Old Version* (2020) Radha Blank's directorial debut partly takes place in this neighborhood, where she plays a forty-year-old aspiring hip-hop artist.

Radha Blank's *The Forty-Year-Old Version*, 2020. *Courtesy of Netflix.*

- *Fresh* (1994) A tale of a young drug courier and how he negotiates the streets and his life with Sean Nelson, Giancarlo Esposito and Samuel L. Jackson.
- *Murder Inc.* (1960) A look at the 1930s Mafia scene starring Peter Falk.
- *The Pickle* (1993) Danny Aiello plays a film director whose latest project is a flop.

BUSHWICK

Located at the top of the borough and leaning close to Queens, Bushwick has been home to several ethnicities, including German, Polish, Irish and Puerto Rican. (Rosie Perez is a hometown heroine!) Several high-priced condos have dotted the area, but it still serves as a backdrop for films with an "old-timey vibe." The gentrification was satirized on *Saturday Night Live* in 2015, with Kevin Hart talking about the new artisanal mayonnaise shop on Bushwick Avenue.

- *The French Connection* (1971) Used as the location for Sal and Angie's Diner at 91 Wycoff Avenue and 912 Broadway for the Santa Claus scene.
- *Malcolm X* (1992) Spike Lee's biopic about the controversial leader filmed at 300 Wycoff Avenue, Myrtle Avenue and Wyckoff Avenue.
- *Ocean's Eight* (2018) The Bushwick United Methodist Church located at 1139 Bushwick Avenue was designed as Lou's (Cate Blanchett) converted loft.

The former site of the Bushwick theater (1396 Broadway), featured here in 1911. *Courtesy of the Brooklyn Public Library.*

- *Passing* (2021) Filming occurred at Bushwick United Methodist Church (1139 Bushwick Avenue) to re-create the interiors of a 1920s Harlem nightclub.
- *The Super* (1991) One of Joe Pesci's first starring films was this misguided effort about a criminally neglectful landlord. The bodega scene was filmed at 1158 Myrtle Avenue.

- *Romeo Is Bleeding* (1994) Gary Oldman is a crooked cop asked to kill a Russian gangster; it is partially set at Myrtle Avenue and Bleecker Street and Myrtle Avenue and Knickerbocker Avenue.

CARROLL GARDENS

For a long time a region filled with Italians, this brownstone-heavy area regularly serves as a backdrop for television and films with a charming family-friendly atmosphere and gob-smacking gorgeous home renovations.

- *Goodfellas* (1990) Jimmy (Robert DeNiro) offers dresses to Karen (Lorraine Bracco) at Smith and 9th Street.
- *I Hate Valentine's Day* (2009) Nia Vardalos (writer and director) plays a flower shop owner at 308 Court Street (it's a martial arts studio now).
- *The Irishman* (2019) One of the last scenes features a significant character killing another character because of a "misunderstanding." The exteriors were filmed at 268 Smith Street.

Court Street in Carroll Gardens, July 2021.

- *Men in Black 3* (2012) Court Street is the spot where Jay (Will Smith) and Kay (Tommy Lee Jones) go back in time to save the world. (Never mind the plot!)
- *Smoke* (1995) Harvey Keitel's character walks past 300 Court Street in the film's last shot.

CLINTON HILL

This small neighborhood is packed with architectural delights and ethnic charm. It is located close to Prospect Heights and filled with lively restaurants.
- *The Intern* (2015) Anne Hathaway plays a perfect tech business owner who owns a perfect home at 383 Grand Avenue.
- *Notorious* (2009) Biggie Smalls's biopic takes place on his home turf of Fulton Street.
- *Munich* (2005) Steven Spielberg's thriller is based on a true story.

COBBLE HILL

Sort of the "kid sister" neighborhood to Carroll Gardens, Cobble Hill is filled with gorgeous homes close to Downtown Brooklyn. Gentrification has elevated this place enough to attract big celebrities.
- *Baby Mama* (2008) A busy perma-single career woman (Tina Fey) improbably hires slacker Amy Poehler to be the surrogate for her child; it includes a scene set in Cobble Hill Park.
- *The Departed* (2006) Jack Nicholson's character hangs out in Fernando's Focacceria at 151 Union Street in place of Boston.
- *Eat Pray Love* (2010) Julia Roberts has a swoon-worthy home on 172 Pacific Street and the former Robin Des Bois café (195 Smith Street at Warren).
- *The French Connection* (1971) The car unloading scene was filmed on Remsen Street.
- *The Girl in the Park* (2007) Stars Sigourney Weaver and Kate Bosworth in a thriller/mystery about a mother who might have found her daughter after she had been missing for fifteen years. Her daughter was stolen from Cobble Hill Park in a scene that is tough to watch.
- *They Came Together* (2014) Upper Sweet Side candy shop, owned by Amy Poehler's character, is located at 254 Baltic Street.

CONEY ISLAND

A part of Brooklyn that embraces its rough-and-tumble past, Coney Island is so important that it has its own chapter in this book.

CROWN HEIGHTS

Located around Atlantic Avenue and the eastern Parkway, Crown Heights was primarily known as the home for Hassidic Jews but is now equally represented by a middle-class Black community.

- *Brooklyn Babylon* (2001) A rapper (Tariq Trotter) falls in love with a Jewish girl (Karen Starc) despite their different backgrounds.
- *Crown Heights* (2017) A drama starring LaKeith Stanfield and Nnamdi Asomugha.
- *Wonderstruck* (2017) Current-day Crown Heights serves as a substitute for 1970s Manhattan (Bedford at Rogers Avenue) in this film, directed by Todd Haynes and starring Julianne Moore and Michelle Williams.

DITMAS PARK

With its location close to Prospect Park, the number of gorgeous Victorian homes and the integration of several ethnic communities, Ditmas Park serves as a vision of New York in the mid-twentieth century but is also filled with restaurants that rival Manhattan.

- *City by the Sea* (2002) Robert DeNiro and James Franco star in this thriller about family, drugs and murder.
- *Next Stop, Greenwich Village* (1976) Underrated Paul Mazursky film (loosely based on his life) about Bohemian life in 1950s New York City.
- *The Pallbearer (*1999) Gwyneth Paltrow was (allegedly) forced by Harvey Weinstein to play the girlfriend of David Schwimmer in this film so that she could play the lead in *Shakespeare in Love*. Schwimmer plays a guy who is the pallbearer for a person he knew in high school he can't remember. A *very* 1999 Miramax film!
- *The Rewrite* (2014) Hugh Grant stars as a screenwriter in a slump living in New York as a writing professor. Outdoor scenes were shot in Ditmas Park.

- *Sophie's Choice* (1984) The exterior of the home at the center of the movie is at 101 Rugby Street.
- *The Squid and the Whale* (2005) Ditmas Park serves as the home for Jeff Daniels's character, who leaves Park Slope to move to the "other side" of the park. "Is that even Brooklyn?" asks his son. Set in the 1980s.

DOWNTOWN BROOKLYN

The center of Brooklyn politics is here, with the Supreme Court Building on Adams Street often serving as a New York City courthouse.

- *Bridge of Spies* (2015) Chambers Paper Fibers on Plymouth Street is the point where Tom Hanks meets his Russian spy and client, played by Mark Rylance in an Academy Award–winning performance, in this Steven Spielberg film. It is based on a true story; the real Colonel Rudolph Ivanovich Abel worked at Ovington Studios in 1953 at 252 Fulton Street.
- *Just Another Girl on the I.R.T.* (1993) The "girl" in this story (played by Ariyan A. Johnson) lives at 224 York Street.

The 78th Precinct of Brooklyn (the exterior for *Brooklyn 99*) at 65 6th Avenue (Prospect Heights), June 2021.

HOYT-SCHERMERHORN SUBWAY STATION

Now a place to catch the A, C or G train, this subway stop has some unused tracks for filming and was famously the backdrop for Michael Jackson's 1987 "Bad" video, directed by Martin Scorsese (along with "Fat" by "Weird Al" Yankovic!).

- *Nighthawks* (1981) Sylvester Stallone and Rutger Hauer are rivals in this thriller.
- *The Pawnbroker* (1964) Rod Steiger plays a Jewish pawnbroker who escaped Nazi persecution and is now dealing with urban violence in New York City.
- *Taking of Pelham 1 2 3* (2009) This would be the remake with Denzel Washington and John Travolta.
- *Teenage Mutant Ninja Turtles* (1990) This is included here for my friend Adam Riske, who loves this film.
- *The Warriors* (1979) The Punks take on our Warriors in overalls and roller skates. Trust me, it's terrifying!
- *The Wiz* (1978) The updated version of *The Wizard of Oz* with Diana Ross.

The Hoyt-Schermerhorn Subway Station. *Creative Commons Attribution/Gryffindoor.*

BROOKLYN BOROUGH HALL

This building was completed in 1848 as the main office for the City of Brooklyn and is located Downtown at 209 Joralemon Street
- *Catch Me If You Can* (2002) Frank Abagnale (Leonardo DiCaprio) puts a scam on Chase bank, filmed here.
- *Mickey Blue Eyes* (1999) Hugh Grant works for an auction house, filmed at this location with co-stars Jeanne Tripplehorn, James Caan, John Ventimiglia, Scott Thompson and Burt Young.

BROOKLYN SUPREME COURT BUILDING

This building was constructed in the 1950s and is often used as a backdrop for TV and film.
- *Sex and the City* (2008) The actual site for the wedding between Big (Chris Noth) and Carrie (Sarah Jessica Parker).
- *American Gangster* (2007) Denzel Washington's character receives justice here.

JUNIOR'S RESTAURANT

- *The Angriest Man in Brooklyn* (2015) Robin Williams plays a man who is dying and wants to live his best life in twenty-four hours. He holds a party at Junior's that is the opposite of fun. (Though, in general, the establishment is terrific.)
- *Ocean's Eight* (2018) A heist is being planned by Sandra Bullock at this location.
- *Sex and the City* (2008) Big (Chris Noth) and Carrie (Sarah Jessica Parker) celebrated their movie wedding at this infamous Brooklyn institution.

DUMBO

The area "Down Under the Manhattan Bridge Overpass" was the setting for movies needing an "urban blight" look. It is now home to artists, wine bars, bike lanes and some of the most beautiful views of Manhattan.

Right: Brooklyn Supreme
Court, 360 Adams Street
(Downtown Brooklyn),
July 2021.

Below: Junior's at 386
Flatbush Avenue,
"Junior's Nite," 2011.
*Creative Commons Zero / Jim
Henderson.*

Down Under the Manhattan Bridge, 2016. *Creative Commons Attribution/Marc Jacobs.*

- *The Amazing Spider-Man 2* (2014) Andrew Garfield plays Peter Parker/Spider-Man in this version, with filming at Anchorage Street and Plymouth Street.
- *Analyze That* (2002) Robert DeNiro and Billy Crystal star in the sequel to *Analyze This*, filmed at the northern end of New Dock Street.
- *The Angriest Man in Brooklyn* (2014) One of Robin Williams's last films took place at 25 John Street.
- *Bridge of Spies* (2015) Spy movie starring Tom Hanks and Mark Rylance. Anchorage Street was remade to look like it did in the 1960s.
- *Broken City* (2013) Ex-cop Mark Wahlberg fights with the mayor of New York City, Russell Crowe, with a scene at Anchorage Street and 135 Plymouth.
- *Coming to America* (1988) In which Eddie Murphy as Prince Akeem woos Lisa (Shari Headley) at Empire Fulton Ferry Park and the River Café.
- *The Dark Tower* (2017) Matthew McConaughey and Idris Elba bring a big-time Stephen King story to life with the Dixie's Pig location at 135 Plymouth Street.

- *Extremely Loud and Incredibly Close* (2011) Tom Hanks and Sandra Bullock star in this movie based on a bestselling novel and filmed at Brooklyn Bridge Park and Manhattan Bridge.
- *I Hate Valentine's Day* (2009) Nia Vardalos's anti-romance comedy was partly filmed on York Street between Washington and Front.
- *John Wick* (2014) Keanu Reeves seeks revenge on his spouse and dog (spoiler!). Filming took place at 26 New Dock Street.
- *John Wick 2* (2017) Keanu Reeves again is being a badass dude (filming at 135 Plymouth Street).
- *Killer's Kiss* (1955) Stanley Kubrick's second movie was partly filmed at Plymouth Street and Adams Street.
- *Morning Glory* (2010) A workplace comedy with Rachel McAdams and Harrison Ford, partly set on Front Street between Main and Dock Streets.
- *New Year's Eve* (2011) One of Gary Marshall's "pay every star $1 million to work for one day" movies had a scene at the corner of John and Jay Streets.
- *Once Upon a Time in America* (1983) Filming took place under the Brooklyn Bridge on Water Street.
- *Paranoia* (2013) A tech billionaire movie with Liam Hemsworth, Harrison Ford and Gary Oldman. Filming took place at Adams Street and John Street.
- *The Pope of Greenwich Village* (1984) Two cousins (Mickey Rourke and Eric Roberts) unknowingly steal from the mob with terrible consequences. Filming took place at New Dock and Water Streets.
- *Rounders* (1998) Matt Damon plays a reformed gambler who returns to poker to save a friend. He parks a truck for "Knish" (John Turturro) at 18 John Street.
- *Safe* (2012) This is not the Julianne Moore movie about toxicity in the environment but a Jason Statham thriller filmed at Plymouth and Pearl Streets.
- *Scent of a Woman* (1992) Lieutenant Colonel Frank Slade (Al Pacino) drives down Plymouth Street between the Manhattan Bridge and the Brooklyn Bridge.
- *She's Gotta Have It* (1986) Nola's apartment is at 1 Front Street (site of Grimaldi's now).
- *Spider-Man 2* (2004) A baby-faced Tobey Maguire in his second film about the webbed teenage hero who fights "Doc Ock,"

played by Alfred Molina. Filming took place at 28 Old Fulton Street.

- *25th Hour* (2002) Spike Lee directed this movie with a bar scene on Water Street.
- *27 Dresses* (2008) Katherine Heigl plans her friend's weddings and secretly hates it, with some scenes shot at 25 Washington Street (near Plymouth).
- *What Happens in Vegas* (2008) Cameron Diaz and Ashton Kutcher get married in Las Vegas and are now trying to figure out married life without each other. Filming took place at Water and Old Fulton Streets.
- *Winter's Tale* (2014) Colin Farrell plays a thief who finds love after thieving in Gilded Age New York City. Also with Russell Crowe, Jennifer Connelly, Matt Bomer and William Hurt. Filming took place at York between Front and Washington Street and Adams Street.
- *Vanilla Sky* (2001) Tom Cruise plays David Aames in this drama directed by Cameron Crowe. Sofia's apartment is at 57 Jay Street at Water Street, and Julie (Cameron Diaz) confronts Aames at Plymouth Street and Bridge Street.

East Flatbush

This is a small, mainly African American community bordering Brownsville and Crown Heights.

- *Above the Rim* (1994) A story about basketball with Leon, Tupac Shakur and Bernie Mac filmed at Samuel J. Tilden High School.
- *The Lords of Flatbush* (1974) Henry Winkler, Sylvester Stallone and Perry King play gang members in 1950s Brooklyn with leather jackets, "ducktails" and loud girlfriends. Exteriors were shot at Samuel J. Tilden High School

Flatbush

Located south of Prospect Park and in the exact center of Brooklyn, Flatbush is a combination of large apartment buildings and Victorian homes. Indeed, it is an intriguing mix of old meets new with several ethnic restaurants to serve your culinary needs.

- *Sophie's Choice* (1983) Stingo, played by Peter MacNicol, lives here.

FORT GREENE

The home of Spike Lee's 40 Acres and a Mule is one of the trendiest and most vibrant sections of Brooklyn, with popular Fort Greene Park and plenty of hipster spots for celebrity sightings. South Portland Avenue, in particular, features some of the most gorgeous brownstones and leafy trees you will ever experience.

- *Brittany Runs a Marathon* (2019) Jillian Bell stars as Brittany who, well…runs a marathon! Written and directed by Paul Downs Colaizzo, it was filmed in Fort Greene at 383 Myrtle Avenue, Claremont Avenue, Park Avenue, Domino Park and 300 Kent Avenue.
- *Brooklyn* (2015) Eilis (Saoirse Ronan) lives with a group of women in a Catholic home on South Portland Ave between DeKalb and Lafayette Avenue.

Subway station in Fort Greene, July 2021.

- *Clockers* (1995) Directed by Spike Lee and starring Harvey Keitel, John Turturro, Delroy Lindo and Mekhi Phifer. The 88th Precinct is at 298 Classon Avenue.
- *Half Nelson* (2006) Ryan Gosling plays a teacher with a drug habit.
- *Munich* (2005) Salameh's apartment is at 259 Claremont Avenue at Dekalb Avenue.
- *Sex and the City* (2008) Miranda (Cynthia Nixon) and Steve (David Eigenberg) get married and move to Brooklyn. The TV series …*And Just Like That* can't change that for many of us fans. Filming took place at 299 Dekalb Avenue.
- *She's Gotta Have It* (1986) The Prison Ship Martyrs Monument in Fort Greene Park is featured on one of her dates.

Gerritsen Beach

This is a tiny sliver of a beach community next to Sheepshead Bay and above Coney Island that Hurricane Sandy almost destroyed in 2012. It is a primarily Irish-Catholic enclave and its own "Cop Town," with a large police and public servant community as residents.

- *The Departed* (2007) "The priests being shamed" scene was filmed at Tamaqua Bar & Marina at 84 Ebony Court.
- *Moscow on the Hudson* (1984) Robin Williams plays a Russian immigrant dreaming of being a U.S. citizen.
- *Shaft* (2000) Samuel L. Jackson's take on the infamous anti-hero from the 1970s; also with Vanessa Williams, Christian Bale, Jeffrey Wright and Toni Collette.
- *She's the One* (1996) Edward Burns directed this romance (as part of his unofficial "Long Island Trilogy") about very basic men who are chased by insanely beautiful women (Jennifer Aniston, Cameron Diaz, Amanda Peet and Leslie Mann).
- *Then She Found Me* (2007) Director Helen Hunt worked ten years to get this novel to the screen.

Gowanus

Located between Park Slope and Carroll Gardens and long known for having an odorous canal, the landscape is now dotted with lofts and coffee shops. The biggest gentrification signifier is a Whole Foods Market on 3rd Avenue and 3rd Street.

- *Half Nelson* (2006) Ryan Gosling plays a teacher with a drug habit.
- *The Irishman* (2019) Under the Brooklyn Queens Expressway by the Smith 9th Street subway substitutes for Chicago.
- *Joker* (2019) With Joaquin Phoenix and Robert DeNiro. The Smith and 9th Street unused subway platform was used as a location.

GRAVESEND

This haunting section of Brooklyn is where you will find a quiet neighborhood filled with the smell of the Atlantic Ocean on rainy days. Annexed to Brooklyn in 1894, it used to be an Italian and Jewish neighborhood but now features a large Russian and Chinese population, among many ethnicities.

- *A Bronx Tale* (1993) Actor Chazz Palminteri wrote the play and screenplay for this story about a young man who is deciding whether to work for the mob. Costars Robert DeNiro and Joe Pesci. Filming took place at Neck Road and East 15th Street.
- *Dog Day Afternoon* (1975) The actual site for the 1972 Chase Bank robbery was at 450 Avenue P.
- *The Godfather* (1972) Clemenza's house was at 1999 East 5th Street ("Don't forget the cannoli!").

GREENPOINT

This neighborhood at the top of Brooklyn has been home to a robust Polish population for decades and is now becoming another artistic hipster haven.

- *Dead Presidents* (1995) A Hughes brothers (Albert and Allen) film about vets coming home from Vietnam and a bank heist. Filming took place at Noble Street and West Street, 69 West Street (intersection of robbery and explosion).
- *The Departed* (2006) Brooklyn substituted for Boston in many scenes in the film, including the Park Luncheonette at 334 Driggs Avenue.
- *Obvious Child* (2014) Jenny Slate plays a young woman dealing with an unplanned pregnancy. Filmed at McGolrick Park at Russell Street and Nassau Avenue.

- *Sleepers* (1996) A Barry Levinson film about a dark tale of abuse has a stickball scene at Franklin and Milton Streets.
- *Vigilante* (1983) A 1980s exploitations film with a grimy look at gangs and drug culture filmed at McCarren Park and starring Robert Forster.

MIDWOOD

This was the location for Vitagraph film company for decades and the home to a sizeable Jewish community. Midwood High School celebrities include Woody Allen, Noah Baumbach, Didi Cohn and Wentworth Miller.

- *Bullet* (1996) Julian Temple directed Mickey Rourke and Tupac Shakur as stars in one of Shakur's last films.
- *Bye Bye Braverman* (1968) Sidney Lumet film starring George Segal and Jack Warden filmed around New York City.
- *The First Wives Club* (1996) Brooklyn College stands in for Middleburg College (2900 Bedford Avenue). Stars Bette Midler, Goldie Hawn, Diane Keaton, Maggie Smith, Sarah Jessica Parker and Stockard Channing.
- The Leading Male. This retail shop (located on Kings Highway at East 12th Street) was the source of the men's disco uniforms in *Saturday Night Fever*. In 1977, John Travolta had the staff bring out polyester suits and shirts located in the basement, which were considered out of style and ready to give back to the vendors. The costuming of the film adds to its allure and iconic status.
- *Malcolm X* (1992) Denzel Washington plays the controversial leader, with filming at East 19th Street.
- *The Purple Rose of Cairo* (1985) Woody Allen's charming ode to the magic of films shot the interior movie scenes at Kent Theater at 1170 Coney Island Avenue. Stars Mia Farrow, Jeff Daniels, Danny Aiello, Milo O'Shea, Dianne Wiest and Edward Herrmann.
- *The Squid and the Whale* (2005) The location of the school talent show was Midwood High School.
- Vitagraph Studios Located at 1277 East 14th Street (near Avenue M).
- *We Own the Night* (2007) Mark Wahlberg and Joaquin Phoenix played a cop and club owner in 1988 fighting the Russian mob. Washington Cemetery is used for a scene.

PARK SLOPE

One of the most venerated neighborhoods in the borough, Park Slope was considered fancy and chic in the mid-twentieth century and later started falling into decay with the "white flight" of the 1960s and the politics of urban planning in New York City until the 1980s. It is now home to many celebrities, including Steve Buscemi, Maggie Gyllenhaal and Patrick Stewart, who Instagrammed his first slice of pizza from the Slope's legendary Smiling Pizza located on 7th Avenue and 9th Street.

- *Addicted to Love* (1997) Meg Ryan and Matthew Broderick filmed this odd love story partially at the Park Slope Armory at 361 15th Street.
- *The Age of Innocence* (1993) Daniel Day-Lewis filmed a scene riding a horse on 8th Avenue between Carroll and President.
- *Alto* (2015) A lesbian romance that is partly set at Slope Fitness at 808 Union Street.
- *Anchorman 2* (2013) Veronica Corningstone (Christina Applegate) lives in a fancy brownstone at 3rd Street at 8th Avenue in this sequel to *Anchorman*.

8th Avenue, Park Slope, April 2022.

- *Awakenings* (1990) The very first scene of this classic film is a snowy wonderland on 7th Street between 7th and 8th Avenues. Stars Robin Williams and Robert DeNiro.
- *Baby Mama* (2008) Tina Fey shops for baby books at Community Bookstore at 143 7th Avenue.
- *The Chosen* (1981) Set in 1944 with two friends played by Robby Benson and Barry Miller. A scene is filmed at a school playground on 8th Avenue and 13th Street.
- *Duplex* (2003) A very odd comedy with Ben Stiller and Drew Barrymore buying a home (240 Berkley Street) that is seen as a money saver compared to Manhattan. Seriously, they buy a duplex in Park Slope in 2003 because it is supposed to be the cheaper option than Manhattan! Did anyone at Miramax read this script first?
- *For Pete's Sake* (1974) Barbra Streisand lives in a lovely apartment at 125 Prospect Park West.
- *Frances Ha* (2012) Greta Gerwig tries to find success as a dancer though she can't dance. Director Noah Baumbach uses locations in Park Slope.
- *Goodfellas* (1990) Michael Imperioli plays Spider, who gets shot by Joe Pesci's Tommy at 94 7th Avenue (interiors filmed here).
- *House on Carroll Street* (1988) Kelly McGillis in a 1950s period piece about the Communist red scare directed by Peter Yates. My friend Patty was interviewed to be her assistant but did not get the job, so I won't see this film.
- *Julie & Julia* (2009) The former Moutarde Café at 235 5th Avenue serves as a Parisian restaurant for Julia and Paul Child.
- *Marriage Story* (2019) More like a divorce story, am I right? Anyway, much was filmed in Park Slope Laundromat (173 7th Avenue), Pino's Pizzeria and the 7th Avenue stop (B and Q trains) at Flatbush Avenue.
- *Meet Joe Black* (1998) Brad Pitt plays "Death" with a crazy "guy hit by multiple cars" scene in a *very* long movie. Filming took place at Park Slope Armory at 361 15th Street.
- *Mr. Jealousy* (1997) Eric Stoltz and Annabella Sciorra play young lovers in Park Slope.
- *Mr. Popper's Penguins* (2011) Jim Carrey plays a rich man who inherits penguins. Carla Gugino plays his love interest, and her home is located at 17 Montgomery Street.

The laundromat from *Marriage Story* at 173 7ᵗʰ Avenue (Park Slope), March 2022.

- *Mr. Wonderful* (1993) Matt Dillon's character lived in Park Slope, and his scenes were filmed on Prospect Park West between 7ᵗʰ and 8ᵗʰ Streets. He and his co-star Mary-Louise Parker were reportedly charming to fans who spotted them.
- *Mistress America* (2011) Greta Gerwig plays a larger-than-life character in this film that she co-wrote with Noah Baumbach and partly filmed in Park Slope on 8ᵗʰ Avenue.
- *Mona Lisa Smile* (2003) A Julia Roberts movie about a bohemian art instructor in the 1950s with a scene at St. Augustine's Catholic Church at 116 6ᵗʰ Avenue.
- *The Muppets Christmas Movie* (2008) You get Muppets and Christmas here. Win/win. Carroll Street.
- *Our Idiot Brother* (2011) A loosely funny Paul Rudd is the brother in question who visits his sister's home at the corner of 1ˢᵗ Street and 8ᵗʰ Avenue.
- *The Royal Tenenbaums* (2001) Margot (Gwyneth Paltrow) moves in with Bill Murray's character (Raleigh St. Clair) at 196 16ᵗʰ Street near 5ᵗʰ Avenue. The home
- *Someone to Watch Over Me* (1987) A romantic thriller starring Mimi Rogers as a socialite with a fancy home at 26 Montgomery Place.

- *The Sorcerer's Apprentice* (2010) Nicolas Cage plays a sorcerer who trains a young man to help him fight his nemesis in a scene at the 7th Avenue F train subway platform.
- *The Squid and the Whale* (2005) The family home takes place at 167 6th Avenue.
- *The War of the Worlds* (2005) The Boston suburbs in the finale of the movie are filmed in Brooklyn with the lead's grandparents at 787 Carroll Street.
- *The Wolf of Wall Street* (2013) Leonardo DiCaprio's British aunt Emma's home is located at 64 Prospect Park West.

BROOKLYN SOCIETY FOR ETHICAL CULTURE

Designed by architect William Tubby for Bon Ami Cleaning Powder inventor William H. Childs in 1900 as a single-family home, this has been the home of the Society of Ethical Culture since 1948. The five-thousand-square-foot home includes a nine-thousand-square-foot garden and has been used for meetings, special events and weddings (including Brooklyn native Rosie Perez in 1999).

- *Malcolm X* (1992) A Spike Lee and Denzel Washington film about the illustrious and controversial leader of the Black Nationalist movement of the 1960s.
- *The Royal Tenenbaums* (2001) Danny Glover's character (Henry Sherman) lives in this beautiful place, and Gene Hackman's character (Royal) asks his wife, Ethel (Anjelica Huston), for a divorce here. It is currently on the market for $30 million.

Brooklyn Society for Ethical Culture, 53 Prospect Park West (Park Slope), March 2022.

THE GRAND PROSPECT HALL

The ornate building (some say garishly so) was bought in 1981 by Michael and Alice Halkias, who became famous in New York for their low-tech but cheery TV ads on New York 1 News promising to "make your dreams come true!" Sadly, Michael died in 2020 of the coronavirus. The Grand Prospect Hall (initially built in 1892) was sold in 2021.

- *The Cotton Club* (1984) Some call this film about the infamous jazz club in 1920s Harlem one of Francis Ford Coppola's most underrated. It stars Richard Gere, Gregory Hines, Diane Lane and Lonette McKee.
- *Prizzi's Honor* (1985) Jack Nicholson and Kathleen Turner play assassins in John Huston's last film. Also with Anjelica Huston, Robert Loggia and William Hickey.
- *The Royal Tenenbaums* (2001) Royal Tenenbaum (Gene Hackman) takes his daughter Margot to lunch here.

The Grand Prospect Hall, 263 Prospect Avenue (demolished in 2022), July 2021.

THE MONTAUK CLUB

The social club was created in 1899 as a place for men to gather, relax and discuss politics. Francis H. Kimball designed it, and the interiors are some of the most gob-smackingly beautiful you will find anywhere in the borough. It is the only social club still standing in Brooklyn, and members enjoy drinking, dining, movie nights, murder mystery–themed parties and events year-round. It is one of the most sought-after places to shoot movies and television shows. It's also an excellent area for celebrity spotting!

- *The Associate* (1996) Whoopi Goldberg and Dianne Wiest star in this comedy about how to be a success on Wall Street.
- *The Chaperone* (2018) A 1920s-era period piece starring Elizabeth McGovern and written by Julian Fellowes.
- *City Hall* (1996) Al Pacino plays the mayor of New York City in this movie, where he gives big speeches.
- *Definitely, Maybe* (2008) A Ryan Reynolds romantic comedy with Brooklynite Rachel Weisz.
- *Gigantic* (2008) Zooey Deschanel at her "manic pixie dream girl" best.
- *Illuminata* (1998) Local John Turturro directed this quirky film with Katherine Borowitz, Beverly D'Angelo, Ben Gazzara and Susan Sarandon.
- *Prizzi's Honor* (1985) Kathleen Turner and Jack Nicholson filmed a party scene here.
- *Q&A* (1990) A Timothy Hutton and Nick Nolte thriller about dirty cops and a young district attorney.
- *Rounders* (1998) Matt Damon filmed a casino scene here and (according to my Facebook group) completely charmed the locals with his smile and friendliness.

ST. FRANCIS RECTORY

Erected in 1904 to serve the Park Slope faithful, the building is gorgeous and ornate. The tower features a twenty-five-note set of Deagan Tubular Tower Chimes.

- *The Departed* (2006) Matt Damon's character's Catholic education as a young man was filmed here as a substitute for Boston.
- *John Wick* (2014) "Little Russia" in Brighton Beach.

Top: The Montauk Club interior, 25 8th Avenue in Park Slope. *Courtesy of the Montauk Club.*

Bottom: St. Francis Xavier Church, 225 6th Avenue at Carroll Street in Park Slope, April 2021.

PROSPECT HEIGHTS

This hipster neighborhood near Prospect Park is basically "brunch central" on the weekends. It is also known for the lovely Brooklyn Museum.

- *Black Swan* (2010) Natalie Portman's character lived at 135 Eastern Parkway (across from the Brooklyn Museum).
- *Ghost* (1990) Oda Mae's parlor/home was at 720 Franklin Avenue, Willie Lopez's apartment was at 592 Prospect Place and scenes were shot at Myrtle Avenue and Broadway, where Patrick Swayze's Sam Wheat chases his killer.
- *The Hot Rock* (1972) The first part of the film takes place at the Brooklyn Museum and the park nearby.
- *Serpico* (1973) Serpico's (played memorably by Al Pacino) first police station is at 653 Grand Street.
- *Vanilla Sky* (2001) 1579 Bedford Avenue is one of the many New York City locations in this Tom Cruise film.

PROSPECT PARK

The second-largest public park in Brooklyn (after Marine Park) was developed by Central Park's landscape architect Frederick Law Olmsted and completed in 1873. It is one of the crown jewels of Brooklyn for both its beauty and the surrounding culture. Actor Montgomery Clift is buried at the private Quaker cemetery located in the park.

- *The Age of Innocence* (1993) Daniel Day-Lewis meets Michelle Pfeiffer's character in Prospect Park, which serves as Boston Park for this film.
- *The Angriest Man in Brooklyn* (2015) Robin Williams's last movie was not exactly a walk in the park mood-wise (the title is a significant indicator of what to expect from his performance), but it does feature a lovely scene in Prospect Park.
- *Goodfellas* (1990) The Prospect Park Zoo (450 Flatbush Avenue) subs for the Tampa Zoo where a debtor is threatened.
- *Highlander* (1986) The "Kurgan" spies on Christopher Lambert and Roxanne Hart as they look at the lions at the Prospect Park Zoo.
- *Illuminata* (1998) Park Slope's John Turturro directed this film about artists at the turn of the twentieth century putting on a play.

Prospect Park West at 3rd Street (Park Slope), October 2021.

- *It's Complicated* (2008) Nancy Meyers movies are romantic and filmed in beautiful places—like the Picnic House in Prospect Park.
- *Radio Days* (1987) Woody Allen's fictionalized version of his life story has a scene at the Prospect Park Zoo where Seth Green's character (our Woody substitute) meets a radio "Whiz Kid."
- *Winter's Tale* (2014) Based on a Shakespearean tale, the 2014 film features Colin Farrell on a horse riding through Prospect Park.
- *The Wolf of Wall Street* (2013) Special effects were employed to make Prospect Park look like London's Hyde Park.

PROSPECT PARK BOATHOUSE AND AUDUBON CENTER

Opened in 1905, the structure on the Lullwater on the Lake in Prospect Park used to be a spot to rent boats and contained a dining room on the second floor when it fell into disrepair in the 1960s. After being preserved as

Ruth Negga in *Passing*, Prospect Park Boathouse and Audubon Center, 2021. *Emily V. Aragones/Netflix.*

a Historic Landmark in 1972, the Boathouse and Audubon Center is now often used as a location belying elegance and sophistication.

- *Bullets Over Broadway* (1994) The Prospect Park Boathouse and Audubon Center is the setting for a wooing scene with John Cusack and Dianne Wiest, who plays Broadway legend Helen Sinclair in an award-winning performance.
- *Passing* (2021) The interiors for the pivotal scene where Tessa Thompson and Ruth Negga, in character, meet for the first time since high school takes place here, which itself "passes" for a hotel in 1920s Manhattan.
- *The Smurfs 2* (2011) The location for a party in a film that stars Neil Patrick Harris is available for weddings and events year-round.
- *Sophie's Choice* (1982) This serves as a picnic site for the leads Meryl Streep, Kevin Kline and Peter MacNicol, who look beautiful.

RED HOOK

For over a century, this was *the* port for Brooklyn and the rough seamen who spent their lives on land there. There are no subways and just one bus that reaches this neighborhood, a combination of new buildings (so much was destroyed there because of Hurricane Sandy) and projects filled with hardworking families. It's also a beautiful spot to watch the Statue of Liberty.

- *Goodfellas* (1990) Early scenes with Robert DeNiro as Jimmy Conway were filmed in Red Hook.
- *Half Nelson* (2006) This Ryan Gosling indie film won a tremendous amount of praise at the time.
- *Last Exit to Brooklyn* (1989) Red Hook is the background for the film based on a famous Hubert Selby Jr. novel.
- *Little Odessa* (1994) A drama about a family of Russian Jews living in Brooklyn.
- *Ocean's Eight* (2018) Sandra Bullock and Cate Blanchett meet in one scene in Red Hook.

Red Hook Pier, April 2022.

Lady Liberty view from the Red Hook Pier, April 2022.

- *Quick Change* (1990) This comedy heist film stars Bill Murray and Geena Davis and is an underrated gem. The "Mexican joust" scene was filmed at 117 Sullivan Street.
- *Red Hook Summer* (2012) Spike Lee's tale of a teenager from Atlanta sent to Red Hook for the summer.
- *Requiem for a Dream* (2000) Harry Goldfarb (Jared Leto) has a scene in Red Hook.
- *Spike of Bensonhurst* (1988) The character of Spike (Sasha Mitchell) hides out in Red Hook to escape mobsters in Bensonhurst.
- *Straight Out of Brooklyn* (1991) The debut film of Matty Rich takes place in a Red Hook housing district.

SHEEPSHEAD BAY

Located by the water and the Shore Parkway, Sheepshead Bay has a beachy feel but a little loneliness that colors the vibe. In addition to being able to buy fishing gear, you will find the best Italian food and Jewish delis that serve restaurants throughout the borough.

- *Brooklyn Lobster* (2005) A family comedy starring Danny Aiello and Jane Curtain as a married couple who own a lobster farm.
- *Glengarry Glen Ross* (1992) The main office is at 1515 Sheepshead Bay Road, and China Bowl Restaurant is at 1520 Sheepshead Bay Road.
- *Goodfellas* (1990) The Bamboo Lounge restaurant is located at 2758 Coney Island Avenue.
- *Shaft* (2000) Samuel L. Jackson reimagines the role of the '70s superhero cop.
- *We Own the Night* (2007) Mark Wahlberg and Joaquin Phoenix star in this thriller set in the 1980s.

SUNSET PARK

This neighborhood borders the historic landmark Green-Wood Cemetery (the final resting spot for artists Jean-Michel Basquiat and Leonard Bernstein) and a waterfront district. It often serves as the setting of urban decline in the mid-twentieth century in films. Writer Hubert Selby Jr. wrote *Last Exit to Brooklyn* about his years involved with sex workers and drugs in the early 1960s based on his experience living there. The area now benefits from the gentrification of surrounding neighborhoods such as Park Slope and South Brooklyn and features the titular named park. It is part of a $1 billion renovation plan in progress.

- *The Departed* (2006) Irish Haven, the bar where Leonardo DiCaprio's character orders a cranberry juice cocktail, can be found at 5721 4th Avenue.
- *Heaven Help Us* (1985) A coming-of-age story set in 1960s Brooklyn with the Hangout Spot at 318 42nd Street and St. Basil's at 352 42nd Street.
- *Joker* (2019) Arkham State Hospital was filmed at Brooklyn Army Terminal, 80 58th Street.
- *Kazaam* (1996) Shaquille O'Neal plays a genie in this odd family film.
- *Out for Justice* (1991) The Pork Chop Shop is at 5205 5th Avenue.
- *Sunset Park* (1996) Rhea Perlman plays a high school basketball coach (really!). It was filmed at Sunset Park High School at 3630 Benson Avenue.

Vinegar Hill

A mere six-block radius makes up this neighborhood located at the East River, the Brooklyn Navy Yard, Nassau Street and Jay Street. Named after the Irish rebellion of 1798, the area used to be called Irishtown due to the primary residents in the early part of the twentieth century being from Ireland. The streets are paved with Belgian blocks (not cobblestones), and you can hear birds chirping in the trees. It's a delight!

- *Tiny Furniture* (2010) Lena Dunham's directorial debut is partly filmed on the streets of Vinegar Hill.

Williamsburg

One of the biggest gentrification stories must be Williamsburg. It has been home to business and manufacturing for well over one hundred years and has a large Hasidic Jewish community. In the early 2000s, hipsters started buying loft space in former office buildings and manufacturing plants, which created a need for bars, bodegas, preschools and nightclubs. Then came the gigantic glass-and-steel condos that took over the area, and now you have a formerly "cool and scary area" changed into Park Slope with more traffic. Progress!

- *American Gangster* (2007) Denzel Washington and Russell Crowe star in this true story about a drug lord.
- *Billy Bathgate* (1991) Dustin Hoffman plays old-timey gangster Dutch Schultz in this 1930s-based drama.
- *Bullets Over Broadway* (1994) One of Woody Allen's most successful comedies was partly filmed here.
- *Coming to America* (1988) Prince Akeem's apartment and the barbershop are at 392 South 5th Street.
- *The French Connection* (1971) Based on a true story about a real drug bust in 1960s New York City (Ellery Street).
- *Garden State* (2004) The Vietnamese restaurant interiors are at 114 North 6th Street.
- *Hitch* (2005) Will Smith and Eva Mendes buy Benadryl at 241 Bedford Avenue, which is a Whole Foods now.
- *I Am Legend* (2007) The Will Smith thriller was filmed at 355 Marcy Street (interiors).

Left: Williamsburg, South 5th Street, summer 2021.

Below: Robert DeNiro and Joe Pesci in *The Irishman*. *Courtesy of Netflix*.

- *The Irishman* (2019) Frank (Robert DeNiro) meets Russ (Joe Pesci) at the Villa di Roma restaurant at 131 Grand Street at Berry Street.
- *John Wick* (2014) John attempts to kill Vito near Peter Luger's steakhouse (178 Broadway).
- *Men in Black 3* (2012) Will Smith and Tommy Lee Jones hang out at the former Relish Diner at 225 Wythe Avenue.
- *Ocean's Eight* (2018) The "rave club" scene is at Marcy Armory, 355 Marcy Avenue.
- *Once Upon a Time in America* (1983) Fat Moe's restaurant is at 95 South 8th Street, and "Noodle's apartment" is at 105 South 8th Street.
- *Quick Change* (1990) The "car honk" sequence takes place at Kent Avenue.
- *School of Rock* (2003) The school interiors were shot at 66 North 6th Street.
- *Serpico* (1973) Al Pacino plays the true story of a cop fighting corruption in the New York City police force.
- *Sherlock Holmes* (2009) Robert Downey Jr.'s first time as Sherlock Holmes had a few scenes filmed in Williamsburg.
- *The Siege* (1998) The Williamsburg Bridge is used in a scene in this Bruce Willis thriller.

WINDSOR TERRACE

This area is long known to be a quiet, working-class Irish neighborhood located to the right of Prospect Park. Windsor Terrace has lovely homes and neighborhood bars, including the famous Farrell's, which had a long-standing policy of not serving women at the bar. Legend has it that superstar Shirley MacLaine (on a date with Brooklyn native son, curmudgeon, writer and enthusiast Pete Hamill), in 1971, was the first to breach this policy.

- *The Amazing Spider-Man* (2012) Aunt May (Sally Field) and Uncle Ben's (Martin Sheen) home is at 36 Fuller Place.
- *As Good as It Gets* (1997) Helen Hunt plays a single mom struggling with a sick child living at 1 Windsor Place.
- *Dog Day Afternoon* (1975) The Chase Bank outdoor shots are at Prospect Park West and 17th Street.

- *I Hate Valentine's Day* (2009) Nia Vardalos wrote another comedy to feature John Corbett and filmed at Windsor Terrace Bagels at 222 Prospect Park West.
- *Turk 182* (1985) A film for Timothy Hutton completists only. Really, the plot here is incredibly lame.

Farrell's

This old-fashioned no-frills Irish bar (mentioned previously) opened in 1933 and is supposedly one of the first places to get a liquor license after Prohibition ended in 1939. It remains a Brooklyn drinking bucket list pilgrimage and is open from 10:00 a.m. to 4:00 a.m. No food is served, and it operates with cash only, but the locals are (sort of) friendly.

- *As Good as It Gets* (1997) Jack Nicholson's character, Melvin Udall, hangs out here in one scene. His character is awful throughout the whole film, but we (the audience) are supposed to think it's endearing.
- *Pollock* (2000) Ed Harris plays the temperamental (and volatile) artist Jackson Pollock, who liked to drink.

Farrell's Bar & Grill (serving women since the early 1970s!), 215 Prospect Park West (Windsor Terrace), May 2022.

DOG DAY AFTERNOON

Enjoy looking through a rack of LPs and playing a video game while you order a Chicago-style dog at this joint. (This is Brooklyn, so, of course, there is a vegan option!) Next, take a walk across the street to see where the original movie was filmed. The super-friendly film-and-pop-culture-obsessed, nerdy staff is here to serve you!

Dog Day Afternoon, 226 Prospect Park West (Windsor Terrace), May 2022.

CHAPTER 10

"ANYONE HERE FROM BROOKLYN?"

Edythe Marrenner was born in 1917 in Flatbush and endured many challenges before her death from a brain tumor at the age of fifty-five in 1975. When she was just seven years old, Edythe was hit by a car and had to endure a body cast in the hot summer sun for several months, which caused her hips to swivel in a particular way that attracted stares.

After a brief modeling career, she went to Hollywood, where the redhead went on to a career playing bigger-than-life characters, earning her five Academy Award nominations under her stage name, Susan Hayward. Highlights include her alcoholic role in *Smash-Up, the Story of a Woman*

Susan Hayward, 1940.
Courtesy of 20th Century Fox.

(1947) to her Oscar-winning tour de force as Barbara Graham (a woman on death row) in *I Want to Live!* (1958) to becoming a gay icon as Helen Lawson in 1967's cult classic *Valley of the Dolls*. ("The only hit that comes out of a Helen Lawson show is Helen Lawson. And that's me, baby!")

During World War II, Hayward enjoyed meeting American troops at dance halls around Los Angeles to support the sale of U.S. bonds. Her introduction at every USO show was, "Anyone here from Brooklyn?"

Hayward had a love/hate relationship with Flatbush but was proud of how tough it made her.

Following is a list of authors, actors, dancers, directors and artists born, raised or settled in the most favored borough of New York City.

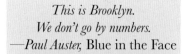

*This is Brooklyn.
We don't go by numbers.*
—*Paul Auster,* Blue in the Face

Paul Auster. *Brooklyn Book Festival 2007/Creative Commons Pictor8.*

Aaliyah (1979–2001), actor and singer
Tatyana Ali (b. 1979), actor
Woody Allen (b. 1935), actor, comedian, director and writer
Lyle Alzado, actor and NFL athlete
Alan Arkin (b. 1934), actor, director and screenwriter
Darren Aronofsky (b. 1969), director, producer and screenwriter
Isaac Asimov (1920–1992), author
Paul Auster (b. 1947), writer and director
Scott Baio (b. 1960), actor
Javier Bardem (b. 1969), actor
Noah Baumbach (b. 1969), director, producer and screenwriter

Joy Behar (b. 1942), actor and comedian
Pat Benatar (b. 1953), singer
Paul Bettany (b. 1971), actor
Radha Blank (b. 1976), actor, director, playwright and screenwriter
Emily Blunt (b. 1983), actor
Joseph Bologna (1934–2017), actor
Shirley Booth (1898–1992), actor
Clara Bow (1905–1965), actor
Lorraine Bracco (b. 1954), actor
Mel Brooks (b. 1926), actor, comedian, director and screenwriter
Foxy Brown (b. 1978), actor and rap artist
Ken Burns (b. 1953), director, producer and writer
Steve Buscemi (b. 1957), actor, director, producer and screenwriter
Rose Byrne (b. 1979), actor
Truman Capote (1924–1984), writer and actor
Bobby Cannavale (b. 1970), actor
Sean Carter aka "Jay-Z" (b. 1969), rap artist and entrepreneur
Joyce Chopra (b. 1936), director
Andrew Dice Clay (b. 1957), comedian and actor

Kim Coles (b. 1962), actor

Didi Conn (b. 1951), actor

Jennifer Connelly (b. 1970), actor

Check Connors (1921–1992), actor

Howard Cosell (1918–1995), sportscaster

Daniel Craig (b. 1968), actor and Bond

Peter Criss (b. 1945), actor and percussionist

Paul Dano (b. 1984), actor

Tony Danza (b. 1951), actor

Larry David (b. 1947), actor, comedian, writer and producer

Mos Def (b. 1973), actor and rap artist

Dom DeLuise (1933–2009), actor and comedian

Neil Diamond (b. 1941), actor, singer and songwriter

Vincent D'Onofrio (b. 1959), actor

Doug E. Doug (b. 1970), actor and comedian

Richard Dreyfuss (b. 1947), actor

Mentally been many places, but I'm Brooklyn's own.
—Jay-Z

Jay-Z, 2011. *Carter Foundation Carnival/ Creative Commons Joella Morano.*

Brooklyn is not the easiest place to grow up in, although I wouldn't change that experience for anything.
—Neil Diamond

Neil Diamond, 1977. *Woburn Abbey/Creative Commons Skybird73.*

Adam Driver (b. 1983), actor

Lena Dunham (b. 1986), actor, director, producer and writer

Jimmy Durante (1893–1980), actor and comedian

"Fab 5 Freddy" (born Fred Brathwaite in 1959), DJ and pop culture icon

Edie Falco (b. 1963), actor

Jimmy Fallon (b. 1974), actor, comedian and TV host

Jerry Ferrara (b. 1979), actor

Lou Ferrigno (b. 1951), actor

Harvey Fierstein (b. 1954), actor and playwright

John Forsythe (1918–2010), actor

Jonathan Franzen (b. 1959), writer

Vincent Gardenia (1920–1992), actor

Paul Giamatti (b. 1967), actor

Jackie Gleason (1917–1987), actor and comedian

Annie Golden (b. 1951), actor and singer
Louis Gossett Jr. (b. 1936), actor
Elliott Gould (b. 1938), actor
Adrien Grenier (b. 1976), actor
Maggie Gyllenhaal (b. 1970), actor, director and
  writer
Buddy Hackett (1924–2003), actor and comedian
Adelaide Hall (1901–1993), singer and actor
Rebecca Hall (b. 1982), actor, director, producer
  and writer
Marvin Hamlisch (1944–2012), composer
Anne Hathaway (b. 1982), actor
Richie Havens (1941–2013), singer and actor
Ethan Hawke (b. 1970), actor, director and writer
Susan Hayward (1917–1975), actor
Rita Hayworth (1918–1987), actor
Lena Horne (1917–2010), actor and singer
Curly Howard (1903–1952), actor and comedian
Moe Howard (1897–1975), actor and comedian

Brooklyn was like Philadelphia made better by its proximity to Manhattan.
—*Jonathan Franzen*

Jonathan Franzen, Time 100 Gala, 2007. *Creative Commons Attribution/David Shankbone.*

I'm from Brooklyn. In Brooklyn, if you say, "I'm dangerous," you'd better be dangerous.
—*Larry King*

Larry King, 2011. *Peabody Awards/Anders Krusberg.*

Shemp Howard (1895–1955), actor and
  comedian
Wyclef Jean (b. 1969), musician
Norah Jones (b. 1979), actor and musician
Gabe Kaplan (b. 1943), actor and comedian
Lanie Kazan (b. 1940), actor
Zoe Kazan (b. 1983), actor
Danny Kaye (1911–1987), actor and
  comedian
Monica Keena (b. 1979), actor
Harvey Keitel (b. 1939), actor
Jimmy Kimmel (b. 1967), comedian and
  television talk show host
Larry King (1933–2021), talk show host
Jemima Kirke (b. 1985), actor
John Krasinski (b. 1979), actor, director and
  writer
Zoë Kravitz (b. 1988), actor
Steve Lawrence (b. 1935), actor and singer
Heath Ledger (1979–2008), actor

Spike Lee (b. 1957), actor, director, producer and writer

Richard Lewis (b. 1947), actor and comedian

Robert Logan (b. 1941), actor

Nia Long (b. 1970), actor

MC Lyte (b. 1970), actor and rap artist

Anthony Mackie (b. 1978), actor

Barry Manilow (b. 1943), singer and songwriter

Debi Mazar (b. 1964), actor

Paul Mazursky (1930–2014), actor, writer and director

Carson McCullers (1917–1967), writer

Anne Meara (1929–2015), actor and comedian

Debra Messing (b. 1968), actor

Alyssa Milano (b. 1972), actor

Arthur Miller (1915–2005), playwright and screenwriter

I come from nowhere, Brooklyn, New York. Williamsburg, Brooklyn. These days, Williamsburg is a hip area, but when I grew up there, the taxi drivers wouldn't even go over the bridge; it was so dangerous.
—*Barry Manilow*

Barry Manilow, 2008. *Creative Commons Attribution/ Matthew Becker.*

I didn't appreciate Brooklyn until I left it.
—*Rosie Perez*

Rosie Perez, Tribeca Film Festival, 2009. *Creative Commons Attribution/David Shankbone.*

Larry Miller (b. 1953), actor and comedian

Wentworth Miller (b. 1972), actor

Isaac Mizrahi (b. 1961), actor, fashion designer and producer

Mary Tyler Moore (1936–2017), actor and producer

Esai Morales (b. 1962), actor

Tracy Morgan (b. 1968), actor and comedian

Errol Morris (b. 1948), director

Emily Mortimer (b. 1971), actor

Charlie Murphy (1959–2017), actor and comedian

Eddie Murphy (b. 1962), actor, comedian, director and writer156

Lupita Nyong'o (b. 1983), actor

Sandra Oh (b. 1971), actor

Mary-Louise Parker (b. 1964), actor

Rosie Perez (b. 1964), actor and choreographer

Rhea Perlman (b. 1948), actor
Harold Perrineau (b. 1963), actor
Michael Pitt (b. 1981), actor
Suzanne Pleshette (1937–2008), actor
Anthony Ramos (b. 1991), actor, singer
    and songwriter
Leah Remini (b. 1970), actor
Matthew Rhys (b. 1974), actor
Joan Rivers (1933–2014), actor, comedian
    and screenwriter
Phoebe Robinson (b. 1984), actor,
    comedian and writer
Chris Rock (b. 1965), actor, comedian and
    writer
Mickey Rooney (1920–2014), actor
Keri Russell (b. 1976), actor
Amy Ryan (b. 1962), actor
Mia Sara (b. 1967), actor
Peter Sarsgaard (b. 1971), actor
Adam Sandler (b. 1966), actor and comedian
Vincent Schiavelli (1948–2005), actor
Jerry Seinfeld (b. 1954), actor and comedian
Michael Shannon (b. 1974), actor and producer
"Judge" Judy Sheindlin (b. 1942), TV personality
Michael Showalter (b. 1970), actor, comedian and director
Gabourey Sidibe (b. 1983), actor

I was bussed to school in Gerritsen Beach in Brooklyn in 1972. I was one of the first Black kids in the history of the school.
    —*Chris Rock*

Chris Rock, 2018. *Courtesy of Netflix.*

I was raised on the streets, in hot, steamy Brooklyn, with stifled air.
    —*Barbra Streisand*

Barbra Streisand, 2007 Clinton "Health Matters" Conference. *Creative Commons.*

Phil Silvers (1911–1985), actor and
    comedian
Tony Sirico (1942–2022), actor
Betty Smith (1896–1972), author
Robert Weston Smith aka Wolfman Jack
    (1938–1995), actor and disc jockey
Jimmy Smits (b. 1955), actor
Wesley Snipes (b. 1962), actor
Paul Sorvino (b. 1939), actor
Morgan Spector (b. 1980), actor
Barbara Stanwyck (1907–1990), actor
Connie Stevens (b. 1938), actor and singer
Patrick Stewart (b. 1940), actor

Jerry Stiller (1927–2020), actor and comedian

Barbra Streisand (b. 1942), actor, director, producer and singer

Marisa Tomei (b. 1964), actor

Michelle Trachtenberg (b. 1985), actor

John Turturro (b. 1957), actor, director, producer and writer

Nicholas Turturro (b. 1962), actor

Mike Tyson (b. 1966), actor and athlete

Eli Wallach (1915–2014), actor

Rachel Weisz (b. 1970), actor and producer

Mae West (1893–1980), actor, comedian and playwright

Michael K. Williams (1966–2021), actor

Michelle Williams (b. 1980), actor

Vanessa Williams (b. 1963), actor and comedian

Patrick Wilson (b. 1973), actor

Shelley Winters (1920–2006), actor

B.D. Wong (b. 1960), actor

I am a dark-skinned, scar-faced dude from the streets of Brooklyn. I can't hide being who I am. It's all over my face.
—*Michael K. Williams*

Michael K. Williams, 2012 Tribeca Film Festival. *Creative Commons Attribution/ David Shankbone.*

157

BIBLIOGRAPHY

INTERVIEWS

Bernstein, Paul. July 20, 2021. Park Slope resident and witness to dozens of films in production on his block from 1975 to 2019.

Grant, Lee. February 16, 2020. Nominated for an Academy Award for Best Supporting Actress in 1971 for *The Landlord*.

Lukasiewicz, Mary. October 25, 2021. Film editor.

Schenkman, Richard. May 20, 2022. Director, producer and writer, *Went to Coney Island on a Mission from God…Be Back by Five*.

QUOTES

Bromley, Patrick. Host and editor-in-chief of *F This Movie* podcast.

Buckley, Robin. *F This Movie* podcast.

DiCristino, Robert. Writer for FThisMovie.com.

Mansfield, Sonia. Co-host of *Dorking Out* and *What a Creep* podcasts.

Meinzer, Kristen. Co-host of *Movie Therapy with Rafer & Kristen* podcast and guest host for NPR's *Pop Culture Happy Hour*, culture critic.

Mintz, Alicia. Co-host/creator of *Trashy Divorces* podcast.

Porras, Margo. Writer of *La Colonia* and co-host of *Book Vs. Movie* podcast.

Powell, Kevin. Poet, journalist, filmmaker, civil and human rights activist, biographer of Tupac Shakur.

Riske, Adam. Writer for FThisMovie.com.

Seymour, Gene. Former film critic at *Newsday* and contributor to *The Nation*, CNN.com and the *Washington Post*.

SECONDARY SOURCES

Amato, Rowley. "Midwood's Historic Vitagraph Studios Gets Wrecking Ball." *Curbed NY*, April 18, 2015.

Auster, Paul. *3 Films: Smoke, Blue in the Face & Lulu on the Bridge*. New York: Picador Henry Holt and Company, 2003.

Badham, John. *On Directing*. Studio City, CA: Michael Wiese Productions, 2013.

Benjamin, Lindsay. "Spike Lee and *She's Gotta Have It* Cast: 7 Ways the Series Updates the Film for Today." *Rotten Tomatoes*, November 20, 2017.

Campanella, Thomas J. *Brooklyn: The Once and Future City*. Princeton, NJ: Princeton University Press, 2019.

Dawson, Nick. *Being Hal Ashby: A Life of a Hollywood Rebel*. Lexington: University Press of Kentucky, 2009.

———. *Hal Ashby Interviews*. Jackson: University Press of Mississippi, 2010.

DeJesus, Jaime. "Scorsese's 'The Irishman' Films Inside Dyker Fixture New Corner Restaurant." *Brooklyn Reporter*, October 23, 2017.

Douglas, Harvey. "Movie Stars Got Start on Flatbush Lots." *Brooklyn Daily Eagle*, February 17, 1933.

Duboff, Josh. "Ed Norton: Spike Lee Taught Me the Secret to Filming in New York City." *Bloomberg*, October 25, 2019.

Dziemianowicz, Joe. "Smoke: The Movie." *Cigar Aficionado*, Summer 1995.

Erish, Andrew A. *Vitagraph: America's First Great Motion Picture Studio*. Lexington: University Press of Kentucky, 2021.

Friedkin, William. *The Friedkin Connection: A Memoir*. New York: HarperCollins, 2013.

Garcia, Sandra E. "The Artists Way: 24 Hours in the Creative Life Radha Blank." *New York Times*, April 22, 2022.

Gordinier, Jeff. "Noah Baumbach Had to Live and Love Before He Made Marriage Story." *Esquire*, December 6, 2019.

Grant, Lee. *I Said Yes to Everything: A Memoir*. New York: Penguin Random House, 2014.

Griffin, David V. "A Sentinel Overlooking Brooklyn Heights Promenade Has Seen Some Ghosts in Its Time." *Brownstoner*, January 15, 2020.

Hale, Mike. "Before Gentrification Was Cool, It Was a Movie." *New York Times*, September 19, 2007.

Helmreich, William B. *The Brooklyn Nobody Knows: An Urban Walking Guide*. Princeton, NJ: Princeton University Press, 2016.

Hubert, Craig. "Film Adaptation of Jonathan Lethem's 'Motherless Brooklyn' Shooting in Brooklyn Heights." *Brownstoner*, February 23, 2018.

Ierardi, Eric J. *Images of America: Brooklyn in the 1920s*. Charleston, SC: Arcadia Publishing, 1998.

Iverson, Kristin. "Back When Brooklyn Was Brooklyn: Director Darren Aronofsky Talks About Brooklyn Filmmaking, and Hubert Selby Jr. at the New Museum." *Brooklyn* magazine, October 1, 2014.

Jewison, Norman. *This Terrible Business Has Been Good to Me: A Biography*. New York: St. Martin's Press, 2004.

Kaufman, Anthony. "Decade: Darren Aronofsky on *Requiem for a Dream*." *Indiewire*, December 1, 2009.

King, Susan. "Joie Lee, Spike Lee's Sister Finds Herself in a 'Mo Better' Place.'" *Los Angeles Times*, August 11, 1990.

Kleeman, Alexandra. "The Secret Toll on Racial Ambiguity." *New York Times*, October 21, 2021.

Krogius, Henrik. *The Brooklyn Heights Promenade*. Charleston, SC: The History Press, 2011.

Lee, Spike. *Spike Lee's Gotta Have It: Inside Guerilla Filmmaking*. New York: Fireside Books, 1987.

Lee, Spike, with Lisa Jones. *Do the Right Thing*. New York: Fireside, 1989.

Lumet, Sidney. *Making Movies*. New York: Vantage Books, 1995.

Major, John, and Ed Lefkowicz. *111 Places in Brooklyn That You Must Not Miss*. Emons, 2018.

Maslin, Janet. "Bringing 'Sophie's Choice' to the Screen." *New York Times*, May 9, 1982.

Moore, Demi. *Inside Out: A Memoir*. New York: Harper Perennial, 2020.

Rooney, David. "'Passing' Film Review, Sundance 2021." *Hollywood Reporter*, January 30, 2021.

Ryan, Hugh. *When Brooklyn Was Queer*. New York: St. Martin's Griffin, 2019.

Silberstein, Rachel. "Darren Aronofsky Returns to Coney Island Alma Mater." *Bklyner*, March 30, 2015

Slide, Andrew. *The Big V: A History of the Vitagraph Company*. Metuchen, NJ, 1987.

Sokol, Tony. "*Once Upon a Time in America Is Every Bit as Great a Gangster Move* as *The Godfather*." *Den of Geek*, September 7, 2021.

Stonehill, Judith, and Francis Morrone. *Brooklyn: A Journey Through the City of Dreams*. New York: Universe Publishing, 2004.

Ugwu, Reggie. "Marriage Story: Autobiographical or Personal? Noah Baumbach Explains." *New York Times*, December 10, 2019.

Wildsam Field Guides. *Brooklyn*. Wildsam Press. 2018

Willmore, Alison. "An Oral History of *Requiem for a Dream*." *Vulture*, October 16, 2020.

Winkelman, Natalia. "Noah Baumbach on Shooting in Brooklyn: 'It's Like a Conversation I'm Having with Myself as a Child.'" BedfordandBowery.com, October 2017.

WEBSITES

Bklyner	Curbed NY
Brooklyn Heights Blog	IMDb
Brooklyn Historical Society	Movie-Locations
Brooklyn Reporter	Newspapers
Brownstoner	Our BK Social

Park Slope Parents
Park Slope Patch
Sidewalk Sherpas
A Slice of Brooklyn

Untapped New York
Vulture
Your Brooklyn Guide

PERIODICALS

Bloomberg
The Brooklyn Eagle
Brooklyn magazine
Brooklyn Paper
Hollywood Reporter

New York Daily News
New York Times
Variety

RECOMMENDED DOCUMENTARIES

Brooklyn Bridge (1981). Ken Burns directed this for PBS.

Coney Island (1991). Ric Burns created this special for the "American Experience" series on PBS.

Easy Riders, Raging Bulls: How the Sex, Drugs, and Rock 'N' Roll Generation Saved Hollywood (2003).

Friedkin Uncut. The director of *The French Connection* with the myths and legends of the filming of the classic movie.

Hal (2018). Amy Scott's exploration of the famed creator Hal Ashby.

I Knew It Was You: Rediscovering John Cazale (2016). The short life and brilliant career of actor John Cazale, who co-starred in *The Godfather* and *Dog Day Afternoon.*

Saturday Night Fever: The Ultimate Disco Movie (2017). An exceptional look at the movie with host Bruno Tonioli (*Dancing with the Stars*).

INDEX

ABOUT THE AUTHOR

Margo Donohue is a longtime Brooklynite who comes by way of the West Coast via San Jose State University. She is a writer, photographer, communications pro and content creator with over twenty years of experience in entertainment, features, films and lifestyle media.

She is the co-host, co-creator, editor and producer of several podcasts, including *Book Vs. Movie*, *Dorking Out*, *Not Fade Away* and *What a Creep*. For several years, she worked in the ancient form of periodicals called "magazines," including *Modern Bride*, *Lucky*, *GQ*, *YM* and *Fitness*.

Filmed in Brooklyn is her first book, and her website is www.BrooklynFitChick. com. On Twitter and Instagram, she is @BrooklynFitChick. You can find her trying to trend on TikTok @margodonohue. A resident of Park Slope, she enjoys hanging out with her cats on her couch and watching far too much streaming TV and movies. Contact her at Brooklynfitchick@gmail.com.

Her top five favorite Brooklyn films are:
- *Do the Right Thing*
- *The Little Fugitive*
- *Moonstruck*
- *Saturday Night Fever*
- *The Warriors*